SUSTAINABLE OPERATIONS AND SUPPLY CHAIN MANAGEMENT

This book takes as its starting point the need to improve sustainability performance across the triple bottom line and reach global sustainable development goals. As such, it places sustainability at the heart of developing and explaining relevant theory, concepts and models in operations and supply chain management. Whereas previous textbooks on operations and supply chain management have focused on augmenting existing models of operations and supply chain management by simply adding on selected sustainability issues, this textbook places sustainability at the heart of operations and supply chain management.

Sustainable Operations and Supply Chain Management consolidates the tools, concepts and methods of operations and supply chain management relevant for reaching sustainable development goals. This book includes not only descriptions of the theories and models but also practical cases based on the most recent developments in different industry sectors, including user electronics, healthcare, fashion and energy. Relevant student exercises are also included for use in the classroom or in personal study.

This book provides an ideal introduction for Bachelor or Masters-level students, whether they are on general management and business degrees, or are focused on areas such as engineering management, technology management or sustainability management. Furthermore, university-level teachers and lecturers will find the material presented in this book a valuable basis for structuring their courses on operations and supply chain management in the context of sustainability.

Melanie E. Kreye is Professor and Chair of Operations and Supply Chain Management at the School for Business and Society at the University of York. She joined the school from the Technical University of Denmark. She further holds an external position at the Manchester Business School, The University of Manchester, UK.

SUSTAINABLE OPERATIONS AND SUPPLY CHAIN MANAGEMENT

Melanie E. Kreye

Routledge
Taylor & Francis Group

LONDON AND NEW YORK

Designed cover image: © Getty Images

First published 2023
by Routledge
4 Park Square, Milton Park, Abingdon, Oxon OX14 4RN

and by Routledge
605 Third Avenue, New York, NY 10158

Routledge is an imprint of the Taylor & Francis Group, an informa business

British Library Cataloguing-in-Publication Data
A catalogue record for this book is available from the British Library

ISBN: 978-1-032-38440-5 (hbk)
ISBN: 978-1-032-38436-8 (pbk)
ISBN: 978-1-003-34507-7 (ebk)

DOI: 10.4324/9781003345077

Typeset in Bembo
by codeMantra

CONTENTS

1

INTRODUCTION

Approaching the subject of sustainability is not an easy task. A vast amount of sustainability-related claims and advertisements have emerged, from new products claiming to be produced with zero carbon emissions to international rankings of the most sustainable countries and from new company slogans to promises of clean transport.[1] Based on these claims and their multitude, sustainability may appear to be well addressed and under control. However, reports increasingly describe the lack of sufficient progress in reducing CO_2 emissions and achieving sustainability targets.[2] Stalled implementation and slow decision-making are often named as the primary reasons for the lack of progress.

Differences and similarities

In examining progress on sustainability efforts, it is striking how different the answer is depending on where you look – both in terms of information sources and in terms of geographic areas (see "Exercise: Polluting countries"). In their analysis of historic CO_2 emissions from 1850 to 2021, Carbon Brief ranked different countries based on their cumulative emissions.[3] Their findings ranked the United States of America in first place (accounting for about 20% of global CO_2 emissions), China in second (11%), Russia in third (7%), Brazil in fourth (5%) and Indonesia in fifth (4%), in close proximity to Germany (4%) and the United Kingdom (3%). Yet, vastly different conclusions can be drawn from different analyses.

Exercise: Polluting countries

What countries come to your mind as the world's big polluters? Why do you associate these countries with pollution?

The World Economic Forum (WEF) posted on LinkedIn in April 2021 that "Denmark is the best performing country for the environment in the world."[4] This statement referred

DOI: 10.4324/9781003345077-1

to the WEF's own ranking, based on the environmental performance index (EPI), which assessed the environmental health and vitality of 180 countries using data from 2020.[5] The EPI is based on a range of performance indicators, including air quality, sanitation, drinking water, waste management, ecosystem vitality pollution emissions and wastewater treatment. The aim of the EPI is to offer a tool to support policy making by identifying where progress has been made and where further action is necessary. The top ten countries according to this ranking are all European countries; the WEF has stated that wealthy countries produce "good policy results" and hence perform better in their ranking. The ranking reflects a subset of environmental effects from the activities performed within the national boundaries of these countries.

Taking a broad view of all production-related activities within a country, Our World in Data annually publishes statistics of per-capita CO_2 emissions. The statistics are based on a country's total emissions divided by its population, indicating the emission contribution of the average citizen within each country. Instead of a ranking, the final product is a colour-coded global map of per capita CO_2 emissions.[6] The results paint a very different picture, with many European countries producing between 4 and 8 tonnes of CO_2 per person. These statistics indicate production-based emissions (i.e., emissions that are produced within a country's boundaries). They exclude any consideration of how products and services are subsequently traded across countries and hence where they are ultimately consumed.

A third statistic for capturing national sustainability efforts is the ecological footprint published by the Global Footprint Network.[7] The ecological footprint is "[a] measure of how much area of biologically productive land and water an individual, population or activity requires to produce all the resources it consumes and to absorb the waste it generates, using prevailing technology and resource management practices" (p. 252).[8] In other words, the ecological footprint captures the total amount of greenhouse gases (GHGs) that are generated by our actions and is thus consumption based. If a product – a mobile phone, a beef steak, or a bunch of flowers – is consumed in Denmark, the ecological footprint of Denmark increases accordingly, irrespective of where this product is produced. The ecological footprint is measured in global hectares (gha) per person and by country includes built-up land, fish footprint, forest product footprint, grazing and cropland. Because trade is global, an individual or country's footprint includes land or sea from all over the world. Each country has a biocapacity per person, which measures the capacity of the ecosystem to regenerate plant matter, and an ecological footprint. Comparison between the two measures allows analysis of whether a country lives above its means (i.e., uses more resources than it replenishes – biocapacity deficit). Combining the measures of all countries provides a global measure of ecological footprint per person, which in 2017 was 2.8 gha per person. This figure can be compared to the global biocapacity, which in 2017 was 1.63 gha per person, meaning that we have a global biocapacity deficit of 1.2 gha.

The ecological footprint is used to determine Earth Overshoot Day: the "day each calendar year by which humanity's demand has used as much from Earth as Earth's ecosystems can renew in that entire year" (p. 252).[9] Earth Overshoot Day can represent all nations' activities – falling on 29 July 2021[10] – or can represent each country's limit based on its ecological footprint in comparison to the global biocapacity of 1.63 gha per person.[11]

TABLE 1.1 Comparison of the sustainability performance of different countries based on different rankings

Country	World Economic Forum ranking based on the environmental performance index[a]		Our world in data statistic	Ecological footprint by global footprint network		
	Rank	Score (max: 100, min: 0)	Per-capita CO_2 emissions[b]	Global hectar (gha) per person[c] global biocapacity of 1.63 gha	Biocapactiy per person	Biocapacity reserve (+) or deficit (−)
Denmark	1	82.5	4.52t	6.9	4.2	−2.7
Luxembourg	2	82.3	13.06t	12.8	1.2	−11.6
United Kingdom	4	81.3	4.85t	4.2	1.1	−3.1
United States of America	24	69.3	14.24t	8.0	3.4	−4.6
Japan	12	75.1	8.15t	4.6	0.6	−4.0
Qatar	122	37.3	37.02t	14.7	1.0	−13.7
China	120	37.3	7.41t	3.7	0.9	−2.8
Brazil	55	51.2	2.20t	2.8	8.6	+5.8
Namibia	104	40.2	1.53t	2.1	6.2	+4.1
Egypt	94	43.3	2.09t	1.8	0.4	−1.4
Basis for evaluation	Results of environmental policies		Production-based activities performed in the national boundaries	Consumption-based activities		

a Based on https://epi.yale.edu/epi-results/2020/component/epi
b Published in 2020 based on data from 2017; available from: https://ourworldindata.org/per-capita-co2
c Published in 2021 based on data from 2017; available from: https://data.world/footprint

Each of these statistics has been measured over multiple years or even decades, allowing us to examine how these values have developed over time. Table 1.1 provides the latest measures for a selection of countries for comparison. This overview illustrates how the different statistics send different messages in terms of the relative ranking of different countries. For example, the WEF ranked Luxembourg second best based on their EPI, while the ecological footprint results rank the same country second worst in the globe, with a country overshoot day on 14 February 2021 (rivalled only by Qatar's overshoot day on 10 February 2021). This contrast demonstrates that the operationalisation of sustainability as a concept and its measurement depends on the viewpoint one takes.

What is sustainability?

There is some consensus around the definition of sustainability. Based on the work of the World Commission on Environment and Development (WCED), convened in 1983 and chaired by the then-Norwegian Prime Minister, Gro Harlem Brundtland, a report was published in 1987 focusing on "our common future," which is now often used as the basis for defining sustainability. The report offered the following definition of sustainable development:

> the development that meets the needs of the present without compromising the ability of future generations to meet their own needs.[12]

> *(p. 54)*

The commission highlighted two main concepts within this definition: needs and limitations (based on technology, social organisation and the environment's capacity). These concepts mirror the measures presented in the ecological footprint above but capture broader concerns, including poverty and hunger. Extending this definition globally leads to the following definition of global sustainability:

> ensuring that all people on this planet have the resources and environment necessary for them to survive and thrive, both now and in the future.[13]

> *(p. XV)*

Based on these definitions, three aspects of sustainability can be highlighted:

- Needs: establishing a contrast to "wants" or "wishes" by defining a global baseline of living standards.
- Limitations: existing limitations imposed by the state of technology, social organisation and biocapacity and their development into the future.
- Intergenerational equality: offering future generations similar levels of quality of life as enjoyed by current generations, requiring long-term thinking and assessment.

Sustainability of what?

Sustainability encompasses a broader view than solely environmental concerns and is typically described through the 3Ps (profit, planet and people), as summarised in the triple bottom line (TBL). The phrase "triple bottom line" was first coined in 1994 by John Elkington, the founder of a British consultancy called SustainAbility. Elkington's argument was that companies should be preparing three different (and separate) bottom lines. One is the traditional measure of corporate profit: the "bottom line" of the profit and loss account. The second is the bottom line of a company's "people account": a measure in some shape or form of how socially responsible an organisation has been throughout its operations. The third is the bottom line of the company's "planet" account: a measure of how environmentally responsible it has been. The TBL thus consists of three Ps: profit, people and planet. It aims to measure the financial, social and environmental performance of a corporation over a period of time. The claim is that only a company that produces a TBL is taking account of the full costs involved in doing business. In his 2018 article, Elkington called for rethinking the TBL, as frameworks developed based on it are predominantly accounting tools that lack the required scale and pace needed to "stop us all overshooting our planetary boundaries."[14]

Profit – Economic sustainability

The first, and traditionally foremost, dimension of sustainability concerns the business case. Initiatives and activities can only be sustainable in the long term if they are profitable or at least do not generate a loss. Performance must lead to economic and financial sustainability in the medium and long term. Typical assessments of financial sustainability focus on achieved profits, cost savings and return on investment.

Planet – Environmental sustainability

The sub-section "Differences and similarities" describes and compares examples of different measures and assessment approaches for environmental sustainability. For initiatives and activities in business, environmental performance is often measured in terms of GHG emissions. In the European Union (EU), GHG emissions are based on the GHG protocol,[15] which enables climate reporting from organisations based on a predefined set of measures and assessment approaches. The GHG protocol was first established in 2001. It breaks emissions down into the following three categories (see also Figure 1.1):

- Scope 1: Emissions caused directly by an organisation's activities, including company vehicles and company facilities.
- Scope 2: Emissions caused indirectly by an organisation through its energy consumption, including electricity and heating.
- Scope 3: All other indirect emissions that are caused along an organisation's value chain. These emissions include upstream activities, such as purchased goods and services, capital goods, fuel and energy-related activities, transportation and distribution, waste generated in operations, business travel, employee commuting and leased assets. Scope 3 emissions also consist of downstream activities, such as transportation and distribution, processing of sold products, use of sold products, end-of-life treatment of sold products, leased assets, franchises and investments.

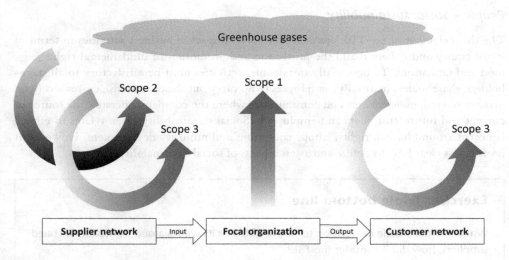

FIGURE 1.1 Emission classification based on the GHG protocol.

As this figure suggests and as we will see throughout this book, much of the GHG emissions arise from the supply chain of a focal organisation through the products they buy, the sources of energy they use, the way their product is being used and so on. Recent attempts have attributed GHG emissions to specific companies – for more information, see the Box "Note: Attributing GHG emissions to companies."

Note: Attributing GHG emissions to companies

In ranking different companies in the fossil fuel area based on their Scope 1 and Scope 3 emissions, the 2017 Carbon Majors Report offered some insightful results on the extent of GHG emissions in the sector. They studied 224 fossil fuel extraction companies and found that they produced 30.6 $GtCO_2e$ (CO_2e stands for CO_2 emissions) in 2015, accounting for about 72% of global industrial GHG emissions. The top 50 polluters in this sample accounted for half of global industrial GHG emissions. Of these 50 top polluters, 29 were oil and gas companies and accounted for one third of global industrial GHG emissions. The sample was dominated by state-owned companies, which represented 59% of all companies in the sample.

The Carbon Majors Database provides data on GHG emissions, particularly related to company activities. This data can form a consistent basis for life-cycle assessments (LCAs). In their 2017 report, the Carbon Majors Database attributed GHG emissions to companies. They stated that "Scope 3 emissions account for 90% of total company emissions and result from the downstream combustion of coal, oil and gas for energy purposes. A small fraction of fossil fuel production is used in non-energy applications which sequester carbon" (Report, p. 5).

Source: *The Carbon Majors Report 2017.* https://cdn.cdp.net/cdp-production/cms/reports/documents/000/002/327/original/Carbon-Majors-Report-2017.pdf?1501833772

People – Social sustainability

The third element of the TBL considers the social impact of business activities in terms of social equity and cohesion and the protection and promotion of fundamental rights (e.g., food and sanitation). To be socially sustainable, activities must be satisfactory to all stakeholders: shareholders (naturally), employees (who carry out the operations), customers (who drive revenues), governments and communities where the company operates (the source of current and future customers and employees). Social sustainability often relates to ethical concerns around human rights, labour conditions and minority development. However, it is often less clear how to define and assess aspects of social sustainability.

Exercise: Triple bottom line

When Walmart made its decision to source 100% of its wild seafood from MSC-certified suppliers, how did it consider the TBL?

Combination and trade-offs in the TBL

Focusing on one of the three elements of the TBL can undermine objectives in one or both other elements. For example, in a briefing first published in January 2021, the European Environment Agency (EEA) highlighted the potential detrimental effects on the environment when continuously seeking economic growth.[16] The briefing emphasised that economic growth often comes at the cost of increases in production, consumption and resource use, worsening the adverse effects on the natural environment and human health. While in the mid-term, many initiatives focused on cost savings can also create positive environmental and social effects (e.g., reduction of material use and improved working conditions), and these initiatives also often create incentives that undermine environmental sustainability. See, for example, the Box "Note: Major European carmakers will hit emissions targets too easily." As it is difficult to globally uncouple economic effects from environmental and social impacts, the briefing by the EEA calls for rethinking the meaning of growth and progress in light of global sustainability.

Note: Major European carmakers will hit emissions targets too easily, research shows

Weak vehicle emissions targets could create an incentive for carmakers to produce more petrol and diesel cars than necessary. Because the emissions targets set by the EU for 2030 can be reached with four years to spare, carmakers may stick closely to a minimum compliance strategy and produce more polluting vehicles, which are much more profitable. This assessment was based on a study by the think tank and campaign group Transport & Environment (T&E) in November 2021. As a result of the car industry's strong commitment to the development of electric vehicles (EV), a gap has emerged between technical developments and sales volume if these are kept in line with EU emissions rules. If these rules are kept unchanged, T&E estimates that an additional 55 million tonnes of CO_2 pollution could be emitted through additional sales of high-emitting sport utility vehicles (SUVs) and hybrid models. Current emission rules could jeopardise the sale of 18 million battery-powered vehicles.

Source: *The Guardian.* https://amp-theguardian-com.cdn.ampproject.org/c/s/
amp.theguardian.com/environment/2021/nov/15/major-european-
carmakers-will-hit-emissions-targets-too-easily-research-shows

---

Criticism and extension of the TBL

The concept of the TBL has received criticism, also by Elkington himself, as it encourages application as an "accounting tool" rather than achieving sustainability performance. While the individual dimensions – economic, environmental and social sustainability – remain the core focus of many sustainability-related initiatives, a fourth dimension has been proposed in the quadruple bottom line. This fourth dimension details cultural sustainability in terms of the purpose of the organisation. Similarly, the quintuple line includes the community process into sustainability considerations. We will revisit some of these additional sustainability concerns that extend beyond the TBL in the concepts of eco-effectiveness, which is introduced in Part I of this book.

UN Global Sustainable Development Goals

Based on the aims of sustainability aligned with the planet and people elements of TBL, the United Nations (UN) adopted the 2030 Agenda for Sustainable Development in 2015. This agenda provides a shared blueprint for peace and prosperity for people and the planet, now and in the future. At the centre of this agenda are the 17 Sustainable Development Goals (SDGs),[17] which connect ending poverty and other social ills with strategies that improve health and education, reduce inequality and spur economic growth, while also tackling climate change and working to preserve the natural environment. In other words, achievement of the goals is interlinked. The SDGs are a call to action and are linked to 169 targets; 3,004 events; 1,251 publications; and 5,366 actions.

Sustainability in context

Despite considerable agreement on the urgency and importance of sustainability, the SDGs are in constant competition with other trends and developments in global society which place additional stress on sustainability. A mega trend is "a general shift in thinking or approach affecting countries, industries and organizations" (p. 3).[18] Mega trends can accelerate or delay the urgency with which we pursue sustainability goals by transforming the social, economic, political and cultural context in which people, companies and institutions are forced to live and do business. The UN describes mega trends as a possible manifestation of human progress or as a sign of failures in policy.[19] Mega trends include demographic change, urbanisation, shifts in global economic power and digital technology (Figure 1.2).

In combination, these trends are expected to result in the following effects[20]:

- Tripling of global consumption by 2050, requiring more products to be made available to a broader set of consumers.
- Creation of consumption centres and scattered rural areas requiring new procurement, transportation, storage and distribution models.
- Need to match the demand and supply of consumer products, including food, due to desertification from climate change.
- Rising availability of new clean technologies for logistics and transport and additive manufacturing, among other processes.
- Potential increase in social inequality and displaced workers through technological change and innovation.

Demographic change

The current global population of 7 billion people is estimated to become 9.3 billion by 2050, with different growth rates in different countries. In addition, populations are expected to age, with the number of people aged over 60 expected to rise from 510 million in 2011 to 1.5 billion in 2050 – a three-fold increase. In parallel, the youth population is expected to decline in Asia from 718 million in 2015 to 711 million in 2030 and further to

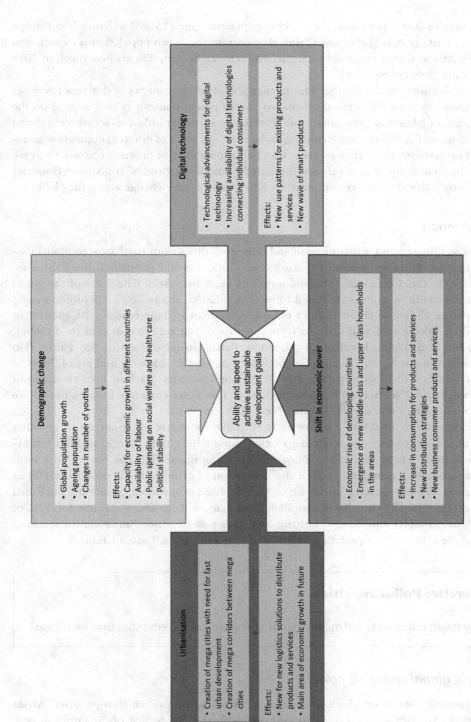

Demographic change

- Global population growth
- Ageing population
- Changes in number of youths

→

Effects:
- Capacity for economic growth in different countries
- Availability of labour
- Public spending on social welfare and health care
- Political stability

Digital technology

- Technological advancements for digital technology
- Increasing availability of digital technologies connecting individual consumers

Effects:
- New use patterns for existing products and services
- New wave of smart products

Ability and speed to achieve sustainable development goals

Urbanisation

- Creation of mega cities with need for fast urban development
- Creation of mega corridors between mega cities

Effects:
- New for new logistics solutions to distribute products and services
- Main area of economic growth in future

Shift in economic power

- Economic rise of developing countries
- Emergence of new middle class and upper class households in the areas

Effects:
- Increase in consumption for products and services
- New distribution strategies
- New business consumer products and services

FIGURE 1.2 Mega trends affecting sustainability.

619 million in 2060. As a result, the working population (aged 15–65) will shrink in Europe and large parts of Asia (Japan and China). In contrast, the youth population is expected to grow in Africa, with a projected increase of 42% by 2030 from 226 million youth in 2015 (19% of the global population).

These developments in demographic change will affect the capacity of different countries and regions for economic growth. Economic development trajectories will depend on the availability of labour and the sustainability of public spending linked to social welfare and health care, which will change according to the evolving needs of different population structures. Furthermore, these changes will affect political stability in different countries – as we saw in the Arab Spring that progressed through the Middle East and North African countries in the early 2010s. Patterns of consumption will fundamentally change across the globe.

Urbanisation

The second mega trend is urbanisation and migratory flows from rural areas to global metropolises. In the early twentieth century, only 20% of world population lived in cities. In the 1950s, this figure was 30%, and now it is more than 54%. The share of the world population living in cities is estimated to be 60% in 2030, and in 2050, 6.5 billion people are expected to live in cities. Further mega cities (urban agglomerations with more than 10 million inhabitants) will arise to complement existing mega cities: Tokyo, Istanbul, Cairo, Mumbai, Delhi, Mexico City, London, Paris, Shanghai, Peking, São Paulo, Rio de Janeiro, Buenos Aires, Teheran, Calcutta, Jakarta, Manila, Moscow and Seoul. Most of these activities will happen in currently developing countries. As Paul Polman (CEO of Unilever) stated, "We have to build as many new cities as we currently have on Earth. We have to build every two months another New York" (p. 96).[21]

The creation of mega cities will result in the development of mega–corridors, or rather communication corridors between mega cities, along which more than 25 million inhabitants will settle. These corridors will not only pose a logistical challenge but will also form the main source of economic growth and generation of gross domestic product (GDP) in these areas. The effect on the environment will likely be tremendous. A recently published study of 167 globally distributed cities suggests that 25 mega cities account for 52% of world's urban GHG emissions.[22] Urbanisation thus poses a major limitation for reaching some of the UN SDGs, especially those related to environmental sustainability.

Exercise: Polluting cities

Why might urban areas and mega cities generate higher GHG emissions than rural areas?

Shifts in global economic power

The economic rise of developing countries – including in Eastern Europe, Asia, Africa and South America – is expected to coincide with the emergence of 300 million new middle-class/upper-class households.[23] This shift will create huge growth potential for products and services with vastly different needs from the current European or Western markets, requiring new distribution strategies and new business models based on low prices, low margins and enormous volumes. Because consumption drives ecological footprint (see sub-section on "Differences and similarities"), this shift in global economic power will create new hubs with increasing ecological footprints under current assumptions.

Digital technology

The rise of digital technologies increases connectivity between individuals through mobile phones, internet use and other connected devices. This digitalisation has driven democratisation of information through collaborative platforms and knowledge-sharing. New archetypes of co-creation and knowledge-sharing will have an impact on all sectors, expanding the potential for not only increasingly sophisticated but also increasingly affordable hardware and the capacity to exploit the information content of big data. Co-creation of information among consumers and making this information available through knowledge-sharing platforms can result in new markets and new use patterns for existing products and services (e.g., car sharing) as well as new waves of smart products. For example, "Digital Factory," "Manufacturing 4.0" and "Industry 4.0" build on intelligence and connectivity as key features of the digital economy.

Sustainability in business

Sustainability is fundamentally a business concern, and companies can profit by understanding and addressing it. If they fail to address sustainability, a company can, at the least, leave money on the table and, at the most, worst jeopardise an entire industry. Think, for example, of the automotive industry and the Volkswagen emissions scandal beginning in 2015. Integrating sustainability issues is not only increasingly important to businesses, but it is also increasingly imperative to ensure business sustainability.

Business sustainability is "the creation of resilient organizations through integrated economic, social and environmental systems".[24] It is based on managing the TBL and enables firms to manage their financial, social and environmental risks, obligations and opportunities. Thus, business sustainability is a means to create resilience of organisations over time through close connections to healthy environmental, economic and social systems, which enable them to respond better to internal and external shocks. As such, business sustainability includes a wider range of variables than the TBL. Based on an in-depth literature review, Ahi and Searcy wrote that these additional variables include volunteer focus, resilience and long-term focus (see also Figure 1.3).[25]

Role of operations and supply chain management in sustainability

"Operations management is the activity of managing the resources that create and deliver services and products" (p. 5).[26] Operations create and deliver services or products by changing inputs into outputs, which in a simplified model can be represented through the "input-transformation-output" process. Supply chain management is the "design, planning, execution, control, and monitoring of supply chain activities" (p. 305).[27] The supply chain focuses on the flow of materials from suppliers to the end customer, passing a network of manufacturers, distributors and retailers, among others. Both operations and supply chain management are therefore concerned with managing resources and their flow (see Figure 1.4 for a simplified overview).

FIGURE 1.3 Business sustainability as an integrated perspective between different variables.

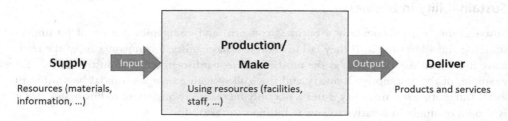

FIGURE 1.4 Input–transformation–output model of operations management within the context of the supply chain.

As sustainability demands a more responsible method of managing resources (see Box "It's time we recognised that overconsuming resources causes climate change and nature's decline"), operations and supply chain management are strongly affected by an increasing orientation towards business sustainability. In addition, operations and supply chain management directly affect the sustainability performance of an organisation. Much of the environmental and social effects organisations impose on their immediate and broader environment are determined by the operations and supply chain management functions. Thus, decisions made by operations and supply chain managers are critical for organisations to achieve sustainability goals and improve sustainability performance.

Box: It's time we recognised that overconsuming resources causes climate change and nature's decline

Carbon emissions are directly affected by the overconsumption and mishandling of resources, including forests, fossil fuels and other raw materials. A report by the UN documented that 50% of the world's carbon emissions and 90% of biodiversity loss are attributable to the extraction and processing of resources. Thus, we need to change the way we approach resources and their management.

Source: https://greenallianceblog.org.uk/2021/03/30/its-time-we-recognised-that-overconsuming-resources-causes-climate-change-and-natures-decline/amp/

The definition of sustainability envisions a more extensive and complex function than the one that traditionally characterises company operations, which is often summarised in the objective of value creation for shareholders. Decision-making processes must be based on the values of responsibility, ethics and sustainability, within a time frame that is consistent with the ability of the system to generate and regenerate adequate resources for sustaining its development. At the centre of many of these decisions are the products and services flowing through the supply chain. In this book, we initially focus our attention on the design of products in light of sustainability (Part I) before investigating operations management (Part II) and finally supply chain management (Part III).

Solutions

Exercise: Triple bottom line

See below for potential answers relating to the individual elements of the TBL.

Profit	Planet	People
• Future profitability of wild seafood based on long-term focus of their business strategy • Different customer segments with higher willingness to pay and higher environmental consciousness • Improved public image of the company	• Improved and long-term sustainability of biodiversity of sourced product • Decreased environmental impact of supply chain	• Selection and diversification of suppliers in terms of small fisheries • Improved working conditions at suppliers

Notes

1 For example, the news headline "Denmark to make domestic flights fossil fuel free by 2030", https://www.bbc.com/news/world-europe-59849898
2 For example, news report "World is failing to make changes needed to avoid climate breakdown, report finds", available from: https://www.theguardian.com/environment/2021/oct/28/world-failing-make-changes-avoid-climate-breakdown-report; and "After 2000-era plateau, global methane levels hitting new highs", https://www.climate.gov/news-features/understanding-climate/after-2000-era-plateau-global-methane-levels-hitting-new-highs
3 Analysis: Which countries are historically responsible for climate change? https://www.carbonbrief.org/analysis-which-countries-are-historically-responsible-for-climate-change
4 https://www.linkedin.com/posts/world-economic-forum_leading-the-world-in-climate-change-commitments-ugcPost-6799317480968900608-tusz/
5 https://www.weforum.org/agenda/2020/06/chart-of-the-day-this-is-the-state-of-sustainability-around-the-world
6 https://ourworldindata.org/per-capita-co2

7 https://www.footprintnetwork.org/
8 Wackernagel, M., Kitzes, J. (2019). Ecological footprint. In *Encyclopedia of Ecology, Five-Volume Set*. pp. 1031–1037. https://doi.org/10.1016/B978-008045405-4.00620-0
9 Wackernagel, M., Kitzes, J. (2019). Ecological footprint. In *Encyclopedia of Ecology, Five-Volume Set*. pp. 1031–1037. https://doi.org/10.1016/B978-008045405-4.00620-0
10 https://www.overshootday.org
11 https://www.overshootday.org/newsroom/country-overshoot-days/
12 Brundtland, G.B., Khalid, M., Agnelli, S., Al-Athel, S.A., Chidzero, B., Fadika, L.M., Hauff, V., Lang, I., Shijun, M., de Botero, M.M., Singh, N., Nogueira-Neto, P., Okita, S., Ramphal, S. S., Ruckelshaus, W.D., Sahnoun, M., Salim, E., Shaib, B., Sokolov, V., … MacNeill, J. (1987). *Report of the World Commission on Environment and Development: Our Common Future*. https://digitallibrary.un.org/record/139811?ln=en:
13 Lefko, M. (2017). *Global Sustainability: How to Do Well By Doing Good*. Morgan James Publishing.
14 https://hbr.org/2018/06/25-years-ago-i-coined-the-phrase-triple-bottom-line-heres-why-im-giving-up-on-it
15 https://ec.europa.eu/environment/emas/emas_for_you/news/news21_en.htm
16 https://www.eea.europa.eu/publications/growth-without-economic-growth
17 https://sdgs.un.org/goals
18 Naisbitt, J. (1982). *Megatrends: The New Directions Transforming Our Lives*. Warner Books, Inc.
19 https://www.un.org/development/desa/publications/report-of-the-un-economist-network-for-the-un-75th-anniversary-shaping-the-trends-of-our-time.html
20 https://www.un.org/development/desa/publications/report-of-the-un-economist-network-for-the-un-75th-anniversary-shaping-the-trends-of-our-time.html; https://www.un.org/development/desa/dspd/world-social-report/2020-2.html
21 Lefko, M. (2017). *Global Sustainability: How to Do Well By Doing Good*. Morgan James Publishing.
22 Wei, T., Wu, J., Chen, S. (2021). Keeping track of greenhouse gas emission reduction progress and targets in 167 cities worldwide. *Frontiers in Sustainable Cities*, vol. 3 (July), pp. 1–13. https://doi.org/10.3389/frsc.2021.696381
23 https://www.mckinsey.com/business-functions/strategy-and-corporate-finance/our-insights/global-forces-shaping-the-future-of-business-and-society
24 Ahi, P., Searcy, C. (2013). A comparative literature analysis of definitions for green and sustainable supply chain management. *Journal of Cleaner Production*, vol. 52, pp. 329–341. https://doi.org/10.1016/j.jclepro.2013.02.018
25 Ahi, P., Searcy, C. (2013). A comparative literature analysis of definitions for green and sustainable supply chain management. *Journal of Cleaner Production*, vol. 52, pp. 329–341. https://doi.org/10.1016/j.jclepro.2013.02.018
26 Slack, N., Brandon-Jones, A. (2019). *Operations Management*, 9th ed. Pearson Education Limited.
27 Gardiner, D., Reefke, H. (2020). *Operations Management for Business Excellence: Building Sustainable Supply Chains*. Routledge.

PART I
Sustainable products

Most people intuitively understand what a sustainable product is. For example, if you are an environmentally conscious consumer, you might want the products you consume to generate less environmental impact than a similar competitive product might. You may also be concerned about the production of this product. Was it produced using ethical employment principles? Were natural resources destroyed to produce or procure parts of this product?

Achieving sustainable products is, however, often difficult. "A rule-of-thumb I give managers is that if your sustainability performance indicators only improve *when customers use your product less often*, it means you're in trouble".[1] Thus, achieving a sustainable product often requires rethinking the product itself to change its production and supply chains.

Exercise: Examples of sustainable and unsustainable products

What examples come to your mind when you think about "sustainable products"? Why do you think these products are sustainable?

What products do you consider to be "unsustainable products"? Why would you describe these products as unsustainable?

Instead of rethinking their products, many companies try to fast-track the achievement of sustainability goals and market their existing merchandise as green products. News of greenwashing[2] frequently appears in popular media (see Box "French advertising body says Adidas is greenwashing" as an example). In an analysis, the United Kingdom's (UK) Competition and Markets Authority (CMA) found that 40% of green claims that have been made online could be misleading consumers because these claims are either vague, based on a brand's own eco logos and labels, or designed to hide or omit contradicting information.

DOI: 10.4324/9781003345077-2

Box: French advertising body says Adidas is greenwashing

France's Advertising Ethics Jury found Adidas guilty of making false and misleading sustainability claims regarding its Stan Smith shoe after handling a case that had been brought in relation to its shoe. Adidas' advertisement reads: "Stan Smith Forever. 100% iconic, 50% recycled." In this case, the complainant argued that the advertisement's claim of the shoe being "50% recycled" was misleading because it could not be clearly interpreted. One possible interpretation is that half of the materials that make up the product are recycled; another interpretation is that these materials can be recycled at the end of their life. The case also argued that the product's "End plastic waste" logo is misleading because buying a product that is partially made of plastic will not end plastic waste.

Source: https://apparelinsider.com/adidas-greenwashing/, published 2nd September 2021; https://internationalleathermaker.com/news/fullstory.php/aid/10277/Ethics_jury_finds_Adidas_ad_is_greenwashing.html, published 1st September 2021.

In response to reports of greenwashing, guidelines for presenting honest claims about products' environmental sustainability have been released. One example is the CMA's Green Claims Code,[3] which details six points for avoiding greenwashing:

1 Claims must be truthful and accurate.
2 Claims must be unambiguous (i.e., they avoid using vague terms or phrases).
3 Claims must not omit or hide information.
4 Claims must make only fair and meaningful comparisons.
5 Claims must be substantiated by evidence.
6 Claims must be based on the consideration of the full product lifecycle (from creation to disposal).

These guidelines for making accurate green claims also enable consumers and regulatory entities to call out greenwashing advertisements.[4] To support honest claims about a product's sustainability, different measures can be used. Table I.1 provides some examples from

TABLE I.1 Example measures for assessing product sustainability[a]

Economic	Environment	Social
Cost/profit	Emissions: CO_2 and greenhouse gases (GHG)	Customer satisfaction
Product quality	Consumption: water, energy (energy efficiency) and hazardous/	Product characteristics
Return on investment	harmful/toxic materials	Health and safety
Market share	Waste generated: recycling and reduction of waste	
	Product durability	

a Based on, for example, Allaoui, H., Guo, Y., Sarkis, J. (2019). Decision support for collaboration planning in sustainable supply chains. *Journal of Cleaner Production*, vol. 229, pp. 761–774. https://doi.org/10.1016/j.jclepro.2019.04.367; Ahi, P., Searcy, C. (2015). An analysis of metrics used to measure performance in green and sustainable supply chains. *Journal of Cleaner Production*, vol. 86, pp. 360–377. https://doi.org/10.1016/j.jclepro.2014.08.005; Yawar, S.A., Seuring, S. (2017). Management of social issues in supply chains: A literature review exploring social issues, actions and performance outcomes. *Journal of Business Ethics*, vol. 141, pp. 621–643. https://doi.org/10.1007/s10551-015-2719-9; Tajbakhsh, A., Hassini, E. (2015). Performance measurement of sustainable supply chains: A review and research questions. *International Journal of Productivity and Performance*, vol. 64, pp. 744–783. https://doi.org/10.1108/IJPPM-03-2013-0056

the academic literature that demonstrate how to make truthful, accurate claims that are supported by substantiated evidence and a transparent process for obtaining values and comparisons.

Solutions

Exercise: Examples of sustainable and unsustainable products

Example answers can resemble the following examples:

Examples of sustainable products	Examples of unsustainable products
• Shampoo bars (instead of liquids packaged in plastic bottles) • Bioplastic (*Trametes versicolor* fungus), which can be used for food containers • Reusable packaging	• Single-use disposable coffee cups • Cigarettes – there are now advertisements on how effective campaigns can keep children from smoking (and drinking alcohol) • Junk foods – these often reduce portion sizes for increased sustainability • Single-use plastic bags for foods such as vegetables • Electronics that are designed to become obsolete

Notes

1 Unruh, G. (2015). The changing business climate is causing product die-offs. *MIT Sloan Management Review*, vol. 57, no. 1, pp. 1–5.
2 Greenwashing makes products seem environmentally sustainable when they are not (to the degree claimed). Greenwashing conveys a false impression or provides misleading information. Greenwashing (also referred to as "green sheen") can also apply to a company's aims and policies.
3 https://greenclaims.campaign.gov.uk/ provides guidance for consumers regarding how to identify greenwashing found under the following: https://www.gov.uk/government/publications/green-claims-code-for-shoppers/green-claims-code-for-shoppers
4 See, for example, the UK advertising watchdog's decision to ban Oatly's marketing campaign due to insufficient evidence: https://www.theguardian.com/media/2022/jan/26/oatly-ads-banned-by-uk-watchdog-over-misleading-green-claims

2

SUSTAINABLE PRODUCT DESIGN

Product design involves imagining, creating and iterating a product that provides value to the end-user by addressing specific needs. In the context of sustainability, product design is therefore the first step in delivering sustainable products to market. As Lobos (p. 145) stated, "Sustainable product design is effectively combining solutions that address environmental issues while elevating user experience and achieving success in the marketplace."[1] As product design connects the earliest life-cycle stages of a product to the consumer, designers play an important role in achieving sustainability by "defining pathways towards sustainable practices and positive wellbeing while delivering design solutions that perform successfully in the marketplace" (pp. 145–146).[2] Before delving into the topic of sustainable product design, it is necessary to define two key terms.

Eco-efficiency and eco-effectiveness

Two core concepts in this chapter and in the remainder of the text are eco-efficiency and eco-effectiveness, both closely connected to the environmental pillar of sustainability. The following definitions are based on the World Business Council for Sustainable Development (WBCSD) 1992 report "Changing course":

Eco-efficiency is achieved by the delivery of competitively priced goods and services that satisfy human needs and bring quality of life, while progressively reducing ecological impacts and resource intensity throughout the life cycle to a level at least in line with the earth's estimated carrying capacity.

Eco-effectiveness positively defines beneficial environmental, social and economic traits of goods and services.

Eco-efficiency essentially means that existing outputs are continuously produced while the company tries to reduce the environmental impact created by their products and operations, for example, through the amount of (and type of) resources used in the process. In essence, eco-efficiency "capture[s] the notion of doing more with less while being environmentally sound."[3] In contrast, eco-effectiveness requires more fundamental changes to

DOI: 10.4324/9781003345077-3

products and their supply chains, aiming at forming a supportive relationship with ecological systems. We will revisit these concepts in further detail in later chapters of this book.

Material choice in product design

One of the most straightforward ways to reduce the environmental impact of a product is by carefully evaluating the material choices. The idea is to replace materials with high environmental impact with materials that are more respectful to the environment, while at the same time reducing the amount of material used (and wasted) through redesigning component structures. This idea has been incorporated in the context of **design for quality**.

In their 1992 publication "Changing course," the WBCSD defined seven principles around the material choices of products with the aim to reduce the environmental impact. These principles have been developed and advanced over the following decades and can be described as follows:

1 Reduce the material intensity of goods and services (i.e., the amount of materials used and incorporated into products and services). This principle ultimately aims at advancing the dematerialisation processes.
2 Reduce the energy intensity of goods and services by incorporating materials that require less energy in their production.[4]
3 Reduce dispersion of hazardous or toxic substances, including heavy metals or persistent organic pollutants (POPs), to minimise chemical risks.
4 Enhance material recyclability by increasing the ability to capture and separate specific materials from the waste stream. Upholding this principle can result in products (and packaging) from which materials, such as plastic and metal, can be easily separated. Such products can provide mid-term solutions to waste-related crises, including the plastic crisis.
5 Maximise sustainable use of renewable resources in products, including the use of renewable energy for the production of these materials.[5]
6 Extend product durability by using materials and material combinations that enable longer use-cycles for products.
7 Increase the service intensity of goods and services.[6]

Over recent decades, companies have invested significant efforts into making their products more environmentally friendly by reducing the environmental intensity of the materials used. Two recent examples of breakthroughs in innovation and development activities are presented below.

Example 1 – Material choice: Lego develops first bricks made from recycled plastic bottles

Toy manufacturer Lego has spent years investigating sustainable alternatives to acrylonitrile butadiene styrene (ABS), the plastic used to produce its iconic bricks. This specific plastic offers the material properties needed for the tight fit and durability of Lego bricks, but it is more difficult to recycle than other plastics, such as polyethylene. In June 2021,

Lego unveiled that they have successfully developed and manufactured bricks made from recycled polyethylene terephthalate (PET) bottles. The company used PET plastic from discarded bottles to produce the standard 4x2 bricks. An average 1-litre plastic bottle can offer enough material for 10 4x2 Lego bricks. The new bricks result from three years of development work, during which time the company experimented with about 250 different variations of materials. The main difficulty was ensuring that these new bricks have the same strength as standard Lego bricks, which was achieved by mixing additives. The company hopes to bring these new more sustainable Lego bricks to the market by including them in new sets by 2023.

Lego has innovated its material use in various other areas as well. A further example is the plant-based resources used for Lego plants. Here, the plastic is made from sustainably sourced sugarcane, which is processed so that the final product looks and feels exactly the same as old Lego plants. Plants from Plants® have been on the market since 2018.

Source: https://www.bbc.com/news/business-57575991; https://www.theguardian.com/lifeandstyle/2021/jun/23/lego-develops-first-bricks-made-of-recycled-plastic-bottles; https://www.lego.com/da-dk/campaigns/plantsfromplants

Example 2 – Material choice: Lafloreparis replaces leather in their handbags

Lafloreparis, a small business founded and run by a daughter-father pair of fashion designers, designs sustainable products by using cork leather, a renewable resource, to replace traditional animal-based leather. The production of animal-based leather leads to negative impacts on the environment by creating residues and emitting these into aquatic ecosystems. Residues include trace-metal, solvents and oils used for cleaning metals from scale, rust and waste water from the dyeing process, which contains salt, excess dyestuff and other chemicals. The use of plant-based leathers aims to avoid these environmental impacts. Lafloreparis uses ethically harvested cork to produce the cork leather used in their handbags. Cork is a renewable resource because it can be harvested repeatedly without harming the tree. Cork oak trees grow in warm regions with dry soil, such as Portugal and Spain. Cork tree forests help protect the biodiversity of their respective regions, as they provide home to endangered species. Harvesting cork requires manual labour by experienced workers. The process motivates a period of new bark growth through which the cork tree increases its absorption of CO_2 while releasing more oxygen. To produce cork leather, the raw material is rolled into thin sheets; dyed with natural, plant-based dyes; and reinforced with a backing material. Through their product design, Lafloreparis also avoids using other environmentally impactful materials, including plastics.

Various other replacement materials for animal-based leather are available and include fungal leather, pineapple leather (used, for example, in Nike's Happy Pineapple range), apple leather and cactus leather.

Source: https://www.lafloreparis.com/pages/our-promise-to-you-eco-friendly-purses; for information on alternative plant-based leather, see also: https://desserto.com.mx/adriano-di-marti-1; https://www.appleleather.com/; https://www.ananas-anam.com/

Material choice offers a first step toward reducing the environmental impact of products. To increase the impact of design choices, designers need to consider the whole product life cycle extending beyond product development. This notion is captured in "Design for X" concepts.

Design for X

Design for Excellence, or Design for X (also DfX), uses *ad hoc* design solutions to anticipate the management of problems linked to business processes for a new product along its production, distribution, use and disposal phases. As Mulder et al. (p. 9) stated, "In order to optimise the performance of a product for a particular life cycle stage, many design approaches are available."[7] These approaches are typically summarised under the umbrella term DfX and have also received attention as "sustainable design," "green design," "ecodesign" or "environmental design." The X in Design for X can represent many possible values related to the product's life cycle, including manufacture, logistics and assembly or disassembly, as illustrated in Figure 2.1.

The different DfX concepts are underpinned by principles that encourage environmentally friendly products, as described in more detail in Table 2.1. These principles can be applied to different DfX concepts to enable environmentally friendlier product designs.

In this chapter, only a subset of DfX concepts that are specifically relevant to sustainability concerns is discussed from among the vast number of concepts explored in the literature. For our purpose, DfX concepts can largely be differentiated into three categories:

1 (Re)designing product characteristics (shaded in dark grey in Figure 2.1).
2 Designing for product use to extend the product use phase.
3 Designing for product end–of–life.

(Re)designing product characteristics

(Re)designing product characteristics using DfX principles focuses on the early life–cycle stages of products, including manufacturing and production. Initial changes in design practices focus on these early product life–cycle stages because of the control manufacturers maintain over these stages and their corporate responsibilities over business practices

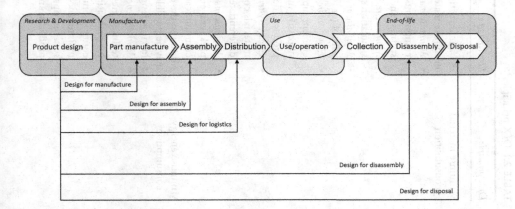

FIGURE 2.1   Exemplary DfX concepts along the product life cycle.

TABLE 2.1 DfX principles[a]

DfX principle	Description
Minimise material consumption	A basic directive is to minimise the amount of material used in products and packaging in general. Design criteria to minimise material consumption include the following[a]:
	• *Minimise material content*: Dematerialise the product or some of its components; digitalise the product or some of its components; miniaturise or avoid over-sized dimensions; reduce thickness; apply ribbed structures to increase structural stiffness and avoid extra components with little functionality)
	• *Minimise residues, scraps and discards*: Select processes that reduce scraps and discarded materials during production; engage simulation systems to optimise transformation processes
	• *Minimise or avoid packaging*: Avoid packaging; apply materials only where absolutely necessary and design the package to be part of (or to become a part of) the product
	• *Engage more consumption-efficient systems*: Design for more efficient consumption of operational materials; design for more efficient supply of raw materials; design for more efficient use of maintenance materials; design systems for consumption of passive materials; design for cascading recycling systems; enable the user to reduce materials consumption and set the product's default state at minimal materials consumption
	• *Engage systems of flexible materials consumption*: Engage digital support systems with dynamic configuration; design dynamic materials consumption for different operational stages; engage sensors to adjust materials consumption according to differentiated operational stages and reduce resource consumption in the product's default state
	• *Minimise materials consumption during the product development phase*: Minimise the consumption of stationery goods and their packages; engage digital tools in designing, modelling and prototype creation; and engage digital tools for documentation, communication and presentation
Minimise energy consumption	Minimise the consumption of energy during the different product life-cycle stages. Depending on the specific product, it may be possible to focus on one or more specific product life-cycle stage(s) for optimising energy use. Vezzoli detailed the following design criteria as examples to achieve these aims:
	• *Minimise energy consumption during pre-production and production*: Select materials with low energy intensity; select processing technologies with the lowest energy consumption possible; engage efficient machinery; use heat emitted in processes for preheating other determined process flows; engage pump and motor speed regulators with dynamic configuration; equip the machinery with intelligent power-off utilities; optimise the overall dimensions of the engines; facilitate engine maintenance; accurately define the tolerance parameters; optimise the volumes of required real estate; optimise stocktaking systems; optimise transportation systems and scale down the weight and dimensions of all transportable materials and semi-products; and engage efficient general heating, illumination and ventilation in buildings

Minimise energy consumption during transportation and storage: Design compact products with high storage density; design concentrated products; equip products with on-site assembly; scale down the product weight; scale down the packaging weight; decentralise activities to reduce transportation volumes and select local material and energy sources

Select systems with energy-efficient operation stages: Design attractive products for collective use; design for energy-efficient operational stages; design for energy-efficient maintenance; design systems for consumption of passive energy sources; engage highly efficient energy conversion systems; design/engage highly efficient engines; design/engage highly efficient power transmission; use highly caulked materials and technical components; design for localised energy supply; scale down the weight of transportable goods; design energy recovery systems and design energy-saving systems

Engage dynamic consumption of energy: Engage digital dynamic support systems; design dynamic energy consumption systems for differentiated operational stages; engage sensors to adjust consumption during differentiated operational stages; equip machinery with intelligent power-off utilities and program product's default state at minimal energy consumption

Minimise energy consumption during product development: Engage efficient workplace heating, illumination and ventilation; engage digital tools for communicating with remote working sites.

Optimise material choice   This principle includes the use of materials with ample supply and low rates of depletion, high potential for recycling and low or no toxicity.

Minimising toxic emissions: Select non-toxic and harmless materials (avoid toxic or harmful materials for product components; minimise the hazard of toxic and harmful materials; avoid materials that emit toxic or harmful substances during pre-production; avoid additives that emit toxic or harmful substances; avoid technologies that process toxic and harmful materials; avoid toxic or harmful surface treatments; design products that do not consume toxic and harmful materials; avoid materials that emit toxic or harmful substances during usage and avoid materials that emit toxic or harmful substances during disposal); select non-toxic and harmless energy resources (select energy resources that reduce dangerous emissions during pre-production and production; select energy resources that reduce dangerous emissions during distribution; select energy resources that reduce dangerous emissions during usage and select energy resources that reduce dangerous residues and toxic and harmful waste)

Use renewable and bio-compatible resources: Select renewable and bio-compatible materials (use renewable materials; avoid exhaustive materials; use residual materials of production processes; use retrieved components from disposed products; use recycled materials, alone or combined with primary materials; and use bio-degradable materials); select renewable and bio-compatible energy resources (use renewable energy resource; engage the cascade approach and select energy resources with high second-order efficiency).

a Based on Vezzoli, C., Manzini, E. (2008). *Design for Environmental Sustainability.* Springer, London, UK. https://doi.org/10.1007/978-1-84800-163-3; Souza, G.C. (2018). *Sustainable Operations and Closed-loop Supply Chain,* 2nd ed. Business Expert Press, New York, NY, USA. https://doi.org/10.4128/9781606493700

(p. 149).[8] Depending on the type of product, designers address these early phases of the product life cycle, where the application of DfX principles – such as saving material and reducing energy use – has the greatest potential effects, because the majority of environmental impact is created there (p. 149).[9] One of the earliest applied concepts is **design for manufacture**. A multitude of industry examples can be found here (see Box: "Example – Design for manufacture: Nike Flyknit"). Further examples include handheld electronics, such as mobile phones, which typically consume the most energy during production. In contrast, household electronics, such as washing machines, consume the most energy during their use phases.

Example – Design for manufacture: Nike Flyknit

In 2012, sports apparel manufacturer Nike introduced a new shoe model, for which the company replaced both the design and manufacturing processes of their product. Rather than assembling a shoe from 37 pieces (as for their Pegasus shoe), Nike developed a new shoe manufacturing system called Flyknit. Using the same technology as sock knitting, Nike knits the entire upper part of the shoe and attaches it to a one-piece injection-moulded rubber sole. This system replaces traditional shoemaking, where various cuts of flat sheets of material – including leather, cloth, fur, rubber and plastic – are laboriously assembled through nailing, stitching and gluing to achieve a 3D shape. This traditional approach results in extensive material waste through off-cuts. Using Flyknit, shoe manufacturing requires no cutting or stitching. This manufacturing approach thus eliminates 50% of manual labour used in the traditional shoe assembly process and reduces scrap pieces of material from cutting. Nike claims that the new manufacturing approach creates 66% less waste than the traditional shoemaking approach.

Source: https://www.bloomberg.com/news/articles/2012-03-15/is-nikes-flyknit-the-swoosh-of-the-future; Sheffi, Y., Blanco, E. (2018). *Balancing Green: When to Embrace Sustainability in a Business (and When Not To)*. MIT Press, p. 224.

A further approach in this first category of DfX concepts is **design for assembly** or **disassembly**. The aim is to facilitate easier assembly and disassembly of a product into its components. The outcome is that components can be more easily separated, recycled or reused. Design for assembly/disassembly incorporates the (dis)assembly cycles that can facilitate the disassembly of similar parts. Vezzoli and Manzini detailed the following design criteria for design for assembly/disassembly[10]:

- *Overall architecture:* Prioritise the disassembly of toxic and dangerous components or materials; prioritise the disassembly of components or materials with higher economic value; prioritise the disassembly of more easily damageable components; engage modular structures; divide the product into easily separable and manipulatable sub-assemblies; minimise the overall dimensions of the product; minimise hierarchically dependent connections between components; minimise different directions in the disassembly route of components and materials; increase the linearity of the disassembly route and engage a sandwich system of disassembly with central joining elements.

- *Shape of components and parts:* Avoid difficult-to-handle components; avoid asymmetrical components, unless required; design leaning surfaces and grabbing features in compliance with standards; arrange leaning surfaces around the product's centre of gravity and design for easy centring on the component base.
- *Shape and accessibility of joints:* Avoid joining systems that require simultaneous interventions for opening; minimise the overall number of fasteners; minimise the overall number of different fastener types (that demand different tools); avoid difficult-to-handle fasteners; design accessible and recognisable entrances for dismantling and design accessible and controllable dismantling points.
- *Engage reversible joining systems:* Employ two-way snap-fit; employ joints that are opened with common tools; employ joints that are opened with special tools, when opening could be dangerous; design joints made of materials that become reversible only in determined conditions; use screws with hexagonal heads; prefer removable nuts and clips to self-tapping screws; use screws made of materials compatible with joint components to avoid their separation before recycling and use self-tapping screws for polymers to avoid using metallic inserts.
- *Engage easily collapsible permanent joining systems:* Avoid rivets on incompatible materials; avoid staples on incompatible materials; avoid additional materials while welding; weld with compatible materials; prefer ultrasonic and vibration welding with polymers; avoid gluing with adhesives and employ easily removable adhesives.
- *Co-design special technologies and features for crushing separation:* Design thin areas to enable the taking off of incompatible inserts by pressurised demolition; co-design cutting or breaking paths with appropriate separation technologies for incompatible materials separation; equip the product with a device to separate incompatible materials; employ joining elements that allow their chemical or physical destruction; make the breaking points easily accessible and recognisable and provide the user with information about the characteristics of crushing separation.

When considering design for assembly/disassembly, designers must often decide between different design alternatives based on environmental concerns. The exercise "Design for assembly/disassembly: Gamma Sound" offers one such analysis.

Exercise: Design for assembly/disassembly: GammaSound

GammaSound has developed two product designs for portable speakers, *UltraLite* and *HighBass*. Based on the following information (each per speaker unit), the company must decide which of the two speaker designs is environmentally better:

1 Resale value of the components (including the costs of transportation to the disassembly facility);
2 Revenue obtained from recycling components that cannot be resold;
3 Processing costs – which include disassembly, sorting, cleaning and packaging; and
4 Disposal costs – including transportation, fees, taxes and processing time.

UltraLite:

Part	Resale revenue (in €)	Recycling revenue (in €)	Processing cost (in €)	Disposal cost (in €)
Printed circuit board	3.50	1.10	2.90	0.00
Laminate back	0.00	0.00	3.60	1.45
Coil	7.80	4.85	5.20	0.00
Processor	8.65	1.90	2.80	0.00
Frame	0.00	0.00	1.90	0.85
Aluminium case	1.35	1.95	2.30	0.00
Total	21.30	9.80	18.70	2.30

HighBass:

Part	Resale revenue (in €)	Recycling revenue (in €)	Processing cost (in €)	Disposal cost (in €)
Printed circuit board	7.25	3.10	1.95	0.00
Coil	6.20	3.90	3.10	0.00
Frame	8.00	0.00	4.25	1.75
Processor	0.00	4.10	2.90	0.00
Plastic case	0.00	0.00	4.20	3.75
Total	21.45	11.10	16.40	5.50

Questions:

1 Which of the two speaker designs is environmentally better?
2 What would happen if there was a change in the supply chain that caused the processing and disposal costs to triple for the laminate back part of the UltraLite?

Note: This exercise is adapted from a similar example presented in Heizer, J., Render, B., Munson, C. (2020). *Operations Management: Sustainability and Supply Chain Management 13th ed.* Pearson, p. 231.

A third DfX concept highlighted here is **design for logistics**. To reduce transportation costs and the environmental impact per unit, design for logistics often aims at reducing packaging or miniaturising the product. Doing so increases the number of products that can be transported on a standard pallet or in a lorry and thus reduces the transportation burden and associated emissions. Another option is the design of reusable packaging, which has an indirect effect through reducing overall product waste. Due to the economic importance of transportation in today's product supply chains, industry examples of design for logistics are manifold, such as the case presented in the Box "Example – Design for logistics (packaging): Walmart."

Example – Design for logistics (packaging): Walmart

In 2006, Walmart rolled out the packaging scorecard, which enables them to measure their suppliers in a sustainability index. On the scorecard, Walmart outlines the following packaging priorities which contribute toward a supplier's sustainability index:

- *Protect the product:* Suppliers are encouraged to design and use packaging that meets International Safe Transit Authority (ISTA) standards for product protection.
- *Reduce materials:* The general directive is to use the minimum amount of packaging. Suppliers should achieve this goal by eliminating packaging components or layers, using "right sizing" packaging and shifting to reusable containers.
- *Maximise recycled and sustainably sourced renewable content:* Suppliers should increase the use of recycled and sustainably sourced renewable content.
- *Enhance material health:* Suppliers should identify if they have priority chemicals in packaging and eliminate them.
- *Design for recycling:* Suppliers are encouraged to design packaging that can be recycled and to work with the Sustainable Packaging Coalition and the Association of Plastic Recyclers toward this goal.
- *Communicate recyclability:* Suppliers should use consumer-friendly recycling labels that meet US Federal Trade Commission standards.

As a response, Walmart's suppliers have engaged in various initiatives to reduce the packaging of their products. For example, Cosco eliminated bulky boxes for their car seats and began to ship them in clear plastic bags instead. Through this redesign, they not only reduced the volume of packaging material and made these products more stackable but also reduced their costs in transport and warehousing. Walmart has followed up on these efforts through multiple renewed initiatives over the years. One example is the company's commitment to reduce plastic waste by encouraging the use of packaging that is recyclable, reusable or industrially compostable.

Source: Sheffi, Y., Blanco, E. (2018). *Balancing Green: When to Embrace Sustainability in a Business (and When Not To).* MIT Press, p. 230; https://corporate.walmart.com/newsroom/2019/02/26/walmart-announces-new-plastic-packaging-waste-reduction-commitments

Design for product use

The second category of DfX concepts described here is concepts that target later product life-cycle phases, specifically the use phase. One of the most widely known (and earliest) examples is when appliance manufacturers started designing products, such as washing machines, with energy- and resource-saving programmes.[11] This approach aimed to reduce the environmental impact of washing machines, 95% of which arises from the use phase of these products. Based on the objective of providing extended product-use cycles, design strategies aim to slow resource loops, create long-life products and design for product life extension. Bocken listed exemplar DfX strategies that fall into this category (Table 2.2).[12] In this chapter, we highlight a selection of the concepts named in Table 2.2.

TABLE 2.2 Exemplar DfX strategies aimed at slowing resource loops

Exemplar DfX concepts to design long-life products	*Exemplar DfX concepts to design*
• Design for attachment and trust • Design for reliability and durability	• Design for ease of maintenance and repair • Design for upgradability and adaptability • Design for standardisation and compatibility • Design for dis- and reassembly

The aim of DfX concepts in design for product use is to factor in considerations of the product's whole life cycle, including life-cycle costs as well as environmental impact, through life-cycle assessments (LCAs) (see also Box "Tool: Life cycle assessment of products"). The fundamental notion is that product obsolescence should be avoided, postponed or reversed.[13]

Tool: Life-cycle assessment of products

Life-cycle assessment (LCA) aims to analyse and measure the environmental impact of a product along its life cycle, including raw material extraction, transportation, manufacturing, packaging and distribution, use by end-consumers and end-of life. LCAs typically provide measurements regarding energy consumption, depletion of minerals and fossil fuels, toxicity and emissions. The assessment guidelines can be found in ISO standards, such as ISO 14040, 14041, 14042 and 14043.

LCAs follow these three steps. First, goal and scope of the LCA are defined, including defining the boundaries of the study, the required level of specificity, and the level of data accuracy. Second, the analysts conduct inventory analysis by collecting and analysing data on the impacts generated through each life-cycle phase. This process can include accessing databases (for common materials and processes). Third, the analysts conduct an impact assessment, through which they assess the contribution to different impact categories, such as energy consumption. Throughout the process, the analysts interpret the assessment, especially for major contributions, for example, through sensitivity analyses.

Performing an LCA provides a company with a better understanding of the major impacts of its products and actions. With this understanding, the company can then implement actions that reduce its environmental impact with the aim to be eco-efficient. We look at the use of LCA again in Part III.

An LCA of supermarket carrier bags by the UK Environment Agency provided some surprising insights. The assessment compared the environmental impacts from the production, use and disposal of typical carrier bags used in UK supermarkets, namely a lightweight carrier made from high-density polyethylene (HDPE), a paper bag, a "bag for life" made from low-density polyethylene (LDPE), a heavier plastic bag with stiffening inserts made from non-woven polypropylene (PP) and a cotton bag.

Each of these bags has a different capacity to carry shopping items due to their size, strength of material and other factors. To make the results of the LCAs comparable, the analysts needed to define the scope for the LCA. Based on a survey of consumer behaviour, the analysts identified that the average shopper in the United Kingdom needed to carry 483 items a month from the shop to their home. A further survey sought to identify packing behaviour among consumers through determining how many items are packed into the different bag options on average. Based on these insights, the analysts collected data points for each of the carrier bags, as shown in Table 2.I.

TABLE 2.I Input data for the compared carrier bag options

Bag type	Volume per bag [litres]	Weight per bag [g]	Items per bag	No. of bags (=483 items/items per bag)
HDPE bag	19.1	8.12	5.88	82.14
Paper bag	20.1	55.20	7.43	64.98
Bag for life (LDPE)	21.52	34.94	7.96	60.68
PP bag	19.75	115.83	7.30	66.13
Cotton bag	28.65	183.11	10.59	45.59

For their calculations, the analysts further defined the system boundaries. The factors they included in their calculation were extraction of raw materials, primary packaging, bag production processes, transportation and end-of-life. The end-of-life options depended on the specific carrier bag and included landfill, incineration and mechanical recycling. Factors excluded from the analysis were inks and dyes, storage at the retailer, capital equipment (e.g., linked to building and facilities) and composting at the end of life. The LCA analysis resulted in the environmental impacts presented in Table 2.II.

TABLE 2.II Environmental impact across the life cycle per bag type

Bag type	Global warming potential across life cycle [kg CO_2 eq]
HDPE bag	1.578
Paper bag	5.523
Bag for life (LDPE)	6.924
PP bag	21.510
Cotton bag	271.533

Source: Souza, G.C. (2018). *Sustainable Operations and Closed-Loop Supply Chain*, 2nd ed., Business Expert Press, New York, NY, USA; https://doi.org/10.4128/9781606493700. Chapter 4; Edwards, C., Fry, J. (2011). Life cycle assessment of supermarket carrier bags: A review of the bags available in 2006. Bristol, UK. https://assets.publishing.service.gov.uk/government/uploads/system/uploads/attachment_data/file/291023/scho0711buan-e-e.pdf

Exemplar design criteria in this category target optimisation of the product lifespan through the following[14]:

- *Design appropriate lifespan*: Design components with co-extensive lifespan; design lifespan of replaceable components according to scheduled duration; select durable materials according to the product performance and lifespan and avoid selecting durable materials for temporary products or components.
- *Design for reliability*: Reduce the overall number of components; simplify products and eliminate weak *liaisons*.
- *Facilitate upgrading and adaptability*: Enable and facilitate software upgrading and enable and facilitate hardware upgrading.
- *Design modular and dynamically configured products to facilitate their adaptability for changing environments*: Design multifunctional and dynamically configured products to facilitate their adaptability for changing cultural and physical contests; design on-site upgradeable and adaptable products and design complementary tools and documentation for product upgrading and adaptation.

An important DfX concept when designing for product use is **design for maintenance**. Design for maintenance "focuses on influencing the future maintenance efforts that are required to keep the product in good condition" (p. 9).[15] When applying design for maintenance, product construction and assembly are typically simplified to enable easy and fast maintenance, including repair or replacement of faulty components.[16] Design for maintenance can include the use of smart components that enable monitoring and hence proactive maintenance instead of repair. Exemplar design criteria when designing for maintenance include the following[17]:

- *Facilitate maintenance*: Simplify access and disassembly to components to be maintained; avoid narrow slits and holes to facilitate access for cleaning; prearrange and facilitate the substitution of short-lived components; equip products with easily usable tools for maintenance; equip products with diagnostic and/or auto-diagnostic systems for maintainable components; design products for easy on-site maintenance; design complementary maintenance tools and documentation and design products that need little maintenance.
- *Facilitate repairs*: Arrange and facilitate disassembly and re-attachment of easily damageable components; design components according to standards to facilitate substitution of damaged parts; equip products with automatic damage diagnostics system; design products for facilitated on-site repair and design complementary repair tools, materials and documentation.
- *Facilitate reuse*: Increase the resistance of easily damaged and expendable components; arrange and facilitate access and removal of retrievable components; design modular and replaceable components; design components according to standards to facilitate replacement; design re-usable auxiliary parts; design refillable and re-usable packaging and design products for secondary use.
- *Facilitate re-manufacture*: Design and facilitate removal and substitution of easily expendable components; design structural parts that can be easily separated from external/

visible ones; provide easy access to components to be re-manufactured; calculate accurate tolerance parameters for easily expendable connections; design for excessive use of materials in places subject to deterioration and design for excessive use of materials for easily deteriorating surfaces.

Modular product designs can advance many of these objectives and typically consist of a set of components, each of which only performs a single function. Modular product designs avoid coupled interfaces between components. The result is that design changes in one component do not require design changes in other components. Modular product designs typically include standardisation through aligning product (part) characteristics, including materials and product dimensions, which simplifies the product portfolio and facilitates sorting and testing.

Despite the predominant focus of DfX concepts on environmental sustainability, social sustainability has also received attention from this community. One term highlighted here is "emotional sustainability," which refers to the human-centred component of design and can drive consumers to use a product for longer.[18]

Product end of life

Product end-of-life concerns have received increasing attention due to the vast amount of waste produced across the world. While end-of-life concerns have traditionally been included in some of the DfX principles described above, we dedicate particular attention to the topic in this sub-section due to the increasing importance in the academic community. See, for example, the latest efforts of Walmart to reduce waste in the Box "Example – Design for logistics (packaging): Walmart."

Design for disposal or design for recycling concerns the use of materials and other resources that can be reused at the end of their life cycle. Design for disposal is closely connected to design for disassembly. The objective is to facilitate the recovery of materials to enable additional use, for example, through recycling. Using materials that are recyclable has certainly attracted increasing attention from product designers and marketeers. However, it has also received criticism related to issues of greenwashing, as described in the Box "A note on recyclable material."

A note on recyclable material

California has tightened regulation on using the arrow recycling symbol on product packaging and aims to ban recycling symbols on products that are not recyclable in practice. In September 2021, the Western US state passed a bill which effectively bans companies from using the arrow symbol unless they can prove that the material is in fact recycled in most California communities and is used to make new products. Prior to this regulatory change, any product could display the symbol, even if the product was not in fact recyclable. This is false advertising, critics say, and as a result, countless tonnes of non-recyclable garbage are thrown in the recycling bin each year, choking the recycling system. The US Environmental Protection Agency estimates that less than 10% of plastic consumed in the US is currently recycled. Instead, most plastic waste is incinerated or dumped in landfills, or shipped overseas. While a global convention bans most trade in plastic waste, waste exports have not yet completely ceased. The argument for restricting the use of the recycling symbol is that having the symbol on product packaging tells consumers that the product is environmentally friendly, when indeed it often is not. Other US states have similarly tightened regulations on recycling systems in hopes of increasing the amount of materials are recycled instead of ending up in landfills.

Source: https://www.nytimes.com/2021/09/08/climate/recycling-california.html

Increasing research and development efforts in companies have resulted in new materials and product designs that aim to reduce the amount of waste generated through their products or reduce the amount of time it takes for this waste to break down. An example is presented in the Box "Example – Design for disposal: Mars Wrigley."

Example – Design for disposal: Mars Wrigley

Mars Wrigley has developed new compostable packaging for their Skittles brand and plans for this packaging to be available to consumers in the US by early 2022. This development is based on a partnership with Danimer Scientific and focuses on a type of polyhydroxyalkanoate (PHA), a polymer product that is made from canola oil. The new material will look and feel the same as plastic but is compostable. The use of eco-friendly packaging such as PHA is currently hindered by cost, as it can be three to five times more expensive to manufacture compared to regular plastic. However, Mars Wrigley will use the new material to replace regular plastic in their packaging, which takes between 20 and 450 years to fully decompose.

Source: https://www-bbc-co-uk.cdn.ampproject.org/c/s/www.bbc.co.uk/news/business-56770732.amp

Creating sustainability through product design

In shifting from efforts towards eco-efficiency to efforts toward eco-effectiveness (see Reminder Box for definitions), product design can function to create sustainability. Sustainability requirements and the attention that is placed on them during the product design phase inevitably extend beyond the product, its materials and its components. These considerations affect the entire product supply chain, including acquisition and procurement, manufacturing and operations, distribution and recovery at the end of the life cycle. Furthermore, these considerations affect the ability to create closed-loop supply chains and a circular economy, topics which are covered in Chapters 9 and 10, respectively.

> **Reminder: Definitions**
>
> **Eco-efficiency** is achieved by the delivery of competitively priced goods and services that satisfy human needs and bring quality of life while progressively reducing ecological impacts and resource intensity throughout the product life cycle to a level at least in line with the earth's estimated carrying capacity.
>
> **Eco-effectiveness** positively defines beneficial environmental, social and economic traits of goods and services.

Many of the concerns that are required for closed-loop supply chains and a circular economy need to be embedded in product design and development through life-cycle thinking. Different approaches to assessing a product's life-cycle impacts are based on the concepts of cradle ("product birth" or conception), gate (release of the product by the product developer to downstream actors) and grave (disposal of a product in a landfill or by incineration based on a linear logic). The resulting approaches to product design are as follows:

- **Cradle-to-gate:** Product designers evaluate the product life-cycle impacts from the extraction of raw materials to the production, packaging and distribution phases. The evaluation of the life-cycle impact stops when the product is released to downstream supply chain actors, such as when the product is delivered to its customers or when it is introduced to the market.
- **Cradle-to-grave:** Product designers evaluate the product life-cycle impacts from development to disposal, extending calculations from cradle-to-gate to include phases linked to the product use and disposal. This approach builds on a linear logic of product life cycles and can include primary and secondary markets of the product.
- **Cradle-to-cradle:** The product's LCA is extended beyond its initial end-of-life (in the cradle-to-grave approach). Instead, the product becomes a useful component for a new product or component, creating a new product life cycle. This notion is the basis for the circular economy (see Chapter 10).

Increasing environmental (and sometimes social) concerns have inspired different industry initiatives to encourage product designers to follow a cradle-to-cradle approach. One of these initiatives is the **Cradle-to-Cradle certification**, which is bestowed by the third-party nonprofit Cradle-to-Cradle Products Innovation Institute.[19] Cradle-to-Cradle Certified® is "the global standard for products that are safe, circular and responsibly made" according to the institute's webpage. The certification requires product designers to meet exacting standards of sustainable design, product circularity and planet-friendly manufacturing processes and comes in various levels from bronze to platinum. In 2021, the first consumer electronics product was certified by the institute (see Box "Example – Cradle-to-Cradle certification: Bang and Olufsen's Beosound").

Example – Cradle-to-Cradle certification: Bang and Olufsen's Beosound

Bang and Olufsen, the Danish producer of audio equipment, received Cradle-to-Cradle Certification® for the Beosound Level, a portable wireless speaker. The product is one of the first to receive the certification and is acknowledged with the Cradle-to-Cradle Products Innovation Institute's bronze-level certification. The speaker applies modular design to enable swapping parts on the product's exterior and interior and hence pushes back against trends of planned obsolescence. For example, modular faceplates allow consumers to self-install a quick refresh to keep the speaker's aesthetics up to date. At the cost of 11,000 DKK (about 1,500 Euro), the brand gives consumers both emotional and logical reasons to hold on to this product. The Beosound Level is also one of the first products to meet the Institute's new Version 4.0 standards, which were introduced in Spring 2021. The Version 4.0 standards include the product's environmental risk and the company's overall sustainable practices in the evaluation.

Source: https://www.architecturaldigest.com/
story/a-bang-olufsen-speaker-designed-to-take-on-the-e-waste-dilemma-launches

---

Solutions

Exercise – Design for assembly/disassembly: Gamma Sound

Question 1:

Revenue retrieval = Total resale revenue + Total recycling revenue − Total processing cost − Total disposal cost

UltraLite = 21.30 + 9.80 − 18.70 − 2.30 = 10.10 €

HighBass = 21.45 + 11.10 − 16.40 − 5.50 = 10.65 €

Insight: After analysing both the environmental revenue and cost components of each speaker design, the design team finds that HighBass is the better environmental design alternative because it has a higher revenue retrieval potential. Note that the team is assuming that both products have the same market acceptance, profitability and environmental impact

Question 2:

Answer: The revenue retrieval from the UltraLite is 21.30 + 9.80 − 25.90 − 5.20 = 0 €. This value is less than the revenue retrieval of the HighBass alternative, which is 10.65 €. As a result, HighBass remains the better environmental design alternative, as it has a higher revenue retrieval potential.

Notes

1 Lobos, A. (2017). Mending broken promises in sustainable design. In J. Chapman (Ed.), *Routledge Handbook of Sustainable Product Design* (pp. 145–159). Routledge.
2 Lobos, A. (2017). Mending broken promises in sustainable design. In J. Chapman (Ed.), *Routledge Handbook of Sustainable Product Design* (pp. 145–159). Routledge.
3 By World Business Council for Sustainable Development, https://www.wbcsd.org/Overview/Our-history
4 The idea of energy use for production is picked up again in Part II.
5 By World Business Council for Sustainable Development, https://www.wbcsd.org/Overview/Our-history
6 The idea of services is picked up in more detail in Chapter 5.
7 Mulder, W., Blok, J., Hoekstra, S., Kokkeler, F.G. M. (2012). *Design for Maintenance.* University of Twente.
8 Lobos, A. (2017). Mending broken promises in sustainable design. In J. Chapman (Ed.), *Routledge Handbook of Sustainable Product Design* (pp. 145–159). Routledge.
9 Lobos, A. (2017). Mending broken promises in sustainable design. In J. Chapman (Ed.), *Routledge Handbook of Sustainable Product Design* (pp. 145–159). Routledge.
10 Vezzoli, C., Manzini, E. (2008). *Design for Environmental Sustainability.* Springer. https://doi.org/10.1007/978-1-84800-163-3
11 Taylor, D. (2017). A brief history of (un)sustainable design. In J. Chapman (Ed.), *Routledge Handbook of Sustainable Product Design* (pp. 11–24). Routledge.
12 Bocken, N. M. P., de Pauw, I., Bakker, C., van der Grinten, B. (2016). Product design and business model strategies for a circular economy. *Journal of Industrial and Production Engineering*, vol. 33, no. 5, pp. 308–320. https://doi.org/10.1080/21681015.2016.1172124
13 den Hollander, M. C., Bakker, C. A., Hultink, E.J. (2017). Product design in a circular economy: development of a typology of key concepts and terms. *Journal of Industrial Ecology*, vol. 21, no. 3, pp. 517–525. https://doi.org/10.1111/jiec.12610
14 Vezzoli, C., Manzini, E. (2008). *Design for Environmental Sustainability.* Springer. https://doi.org/10.1007/978-1-84800-163-3
15 Mulder, W., Blok, J., Hoekstra, S., Kokkeler, F.G.M. (2012). *Design for Maintenance.* University of Twente.
16 We will reflect more on product maintenance and its role in sustainability in Chapter 6.
17 Vezzoli, C., Manzini, E. (2008). *Design for Environmental Sustainability.* Springer. https://doi.org/10.1007/978-1-84800-163-3
18 For more details, please see references, including Chapman, J. (2009). Design for (emotional) durability, *Design Issues*, vol. 25, no. 4, pp. 29–35 and the *Routledge Handbook of Sustainable Product Design*, Chapter 18.
19 https://www.c2ccertified.org/

CASE 1

Sustainable product design at Ambu A/S

Integrating environmental sustainability into the manufactured devices at Ambu A/S requires fundamental changes in the design process. The company provides single-use medical devices, such as single-use endoscopes, a product the company pioneered in 2009 and which defines their global competitiveness to date. The current aim of Ambu A/S is to integrate a circular economy into the company's products and processes. Questions that demand attention in this context include not only whether single-use devices represent the way forward but also what innovations in material use can reduce the company's impact on the environment.

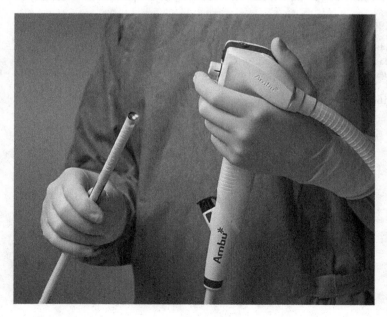

FIGURE C1.1 Single-use gastroenterological endoscope.

DOI: 10.4324/9781003345077-4

Background

Ambu A/S is an engineering company operating in the healthcare sector. Founded in 1937, Ambu currently employs more than 4,500 employees worldwide, with innovation centres in Germany, China, Malaysia, the USA and Denmark and production plants in China, Malaysia, the USA and soon in Mexico. They design, develop and manufacture single-use medical devices for healthcare professionals in three business areas. First, they provide devices for visualisation, including their award-winning single-use endoscope, which can be used for diagnosis. Second, Ambu provides devices for airway management and anaesthesia, including face masks, breathing bags and resuscitators. Third, the company provides devices for patient monitoring and diagnostics, including sensors attached to the patient to monitor vitals including heartbeat and brain activity. The company takes pride in providing high-quality and safe solutions based on the latest breakthrough technology in material use and functioning. Two of their designs for single-use endoscopes won the Red Dot design awards in 2021, acknowledging the innovativeness of the company and the quality and ergonomics of their products.[1]

Environmental commitment

Ambu has committed to environmental sustainability and has implemented various related organisational initiatives. The company has a dedicated sustainability department, which impacts the entire value chain. In addition, commitment to the UN's Sustainable Development Goals is embedded in all Ambu projects, and the company documents its progress in annual sustainability reports to ensure accountability and transparency. Ambu has also established various external partnerships aimed at reducing the impact of plastic waste on the environment. For example, through their commitment to the Operation Clean Sweep initiative, Ambu has worked to prevent plastic pellets, flakes and powders used in product manufacturing from ending up in nature and waterways.

Translating these commitments into tangible objectives for the near future, Ambu has defined the following environmental design goals for their products:

- 100% phthalate-free products by 2020 (achieved): Phthalates or plasticisers are chemicals that are added to many plastics to make them more durable and thereby create problems in landfills due to slow degradation. Some phthalates can have detrimental health effects for humans and animals.
- 95% of new products released after 2025 will be PVC-free.
- 100% recyclable, reusable or compostable packaging by 2025.

In sum, these goals will help Ambu to become more environmentally sustainable. In addition, Ambu is investigating phasing-in materials with bio-based or recycled content (from advanced/chemical recycling) and developing partnerships that will enable the take-back and recycling of single-use medical devices in order to give new life to the materials used in the healthcare system.

Challenges in the healthcare industry

Operating in the healthcare industry places high demands on Ambu and its products, resulting in clear benefits for single-use equipment (Table C1.1). In contrast, designing and preparing equipment for multi-use may not necessarily result in environmental benefits. For example, reusable equipment requires additional products (often made of single-use plastic), including face shields, a long-sleeved gown, examination gloves, shoe covers and materials for cleaning (e.g., cloth, wipes, syringe, water and chemicals). In a comparative study undertaken by Sørensen and Grüttner, the authors found that comparison between single-use and multi-use bronchoscopes must consider energy consumption, CO_2 emissions and the value of scarce resources and energy created through incineration, among other factors, to properly evaluate environmental benefits.[2] Depending on the focus of the analysis, multi-use equipment creates net CO_2 emission benefits when at least two endoscopes are cleaned per reprocessing procedure. Thus, replacing single-use endoscopes would be beneficial for the CO_2 balance in cases where one to two multi-use endoscopes are cleaned at a time.

An important concern in the healthcare sector is the high level of regulations and certifications needed to ensure that products used by healthcare professionals are safe. Approval by national/international agencies depends upon factors including materials used, product performance and transportation. For example, in the European Union (EU), medical devices that have come in contact with bodily fluids (such as through placing over a patient's mouth and nose) must be handled in accordance with the guidelines on hazardous waste. Compliance reduces the risk of contamination. In sum, regulations determine what products can be marketed in the healthcare sector and often how they must be handled for disposal.

A circular design guide, a design tool for the engineers

To support their journey towards increased environmental sustainability through circular design, Ambu is shifting their design and product development processes to incorporate environmental concerns into the earliest stages of a product's life cycle. They aim to design their products with consideration to the product life cycle, for example, keeping materials at their highest value when reusing or recycling. The *circular design guide* defines six focus areas in which to support new innovation projects that seek to make products fit for a circular economy. The design guide is a framework for boosting the awareness and understanding of sustainability in product design. The guide is used both in the training of employees and in implementing sustainability as part of the innovation process such that all projects will have

TABLE C1.1 Benefits of single-use and multi-use equipment

Benefits of single use	*Benefits of multiple use*
Sterile straight from pack	Potential reduction of waste sent to
High availability of the devices	incineration or landfills
Improved workflow for healthcare professionals	Reduced GHG emissions through
Eliminates risk of cross-contamination	reduced material production and
Eliminates reprocessing of multi-use equipment including	reduced energy production
chemicals and plastic	
Consistent high quality and performance	
Low cost across the supply chain	

to set ambitions based on one or more of the focus areas. To measure performance and progress in circularity or environmental sustainability, it is important to include measures related to the product design. During 2020–2021, Ambu developed a focus on understanding their products from a sustainability perspective. As part of this focus, they have completed a flow analysis of the materials used in their products. The analysis includes sustainability indicators such as recycled content and the ability to recycle. This work will enable the company to make more informed decisions on shaping future innovation to be more sustainable.

Notes

1 https://www.ambu.com/Files/Files/Ambu/Investor/News/English/2021/Press-release_Red-DotAwards2021.pdf
2 Sørensen, B. L., Grüttner, H. (2018). Comparative study on environmental impacts of reusable and single-use bronchoscopes. *American Journal of Environmental Protection*, vol. 7, no. 4, pp. 55–62. https://doi.org/10.11648/j.ajep.20180704.11

PART II
Sustainability and operations

Operations management is "the activity of managing the resources that create and deliver services and products" (p. 5).[1] This is done via the transformation of inputs into outputs. The management of the complex system of labour, machinery, resource materials and knowledge is defined as the operating system. Operations management is relevant for organisations across industry sectors. It applies to a restaurant as much as to an automotive manufacturer or a law firm. It also applies to organisations in the private and public sectors alike, although the majority of examples and concepts described in this section apply predominantly to for-profit organisations.

Operations management focuses on the management of resources with the aim to improve resource efficiency (i.e., the use of the smallest amount of resources to produce the same level of output). Operations management refers to how resources are being used and is hence directly linked to sustainability. The European Commission phrases it as follows:

> If we carry on using resources at the current rate, by 2050 we will need, on aggregate, the equivalent of more than two planets to sustain us, and the aspirations of many for a better quality of life will not be achieved.[2]

Not all efforts to achieve resource efficiency connect equally to all three pillars of the triple bottom line. Greenhouse gas (GHG) emissions from global industry accounted for just over 30% of global GHG emissions in 2010 (IPCC report, p. 802).[3] Industry-related GHG emissions have continued to increase and are higher than GHG emissions from other sectors. GHG emissions grew from 10.4 $GtCO_2eq$ in 1990 to 13.0 $GtCO_2eq$ in 2005 to 15.4 $GtCO_2eq$ in 2010.[4] Values from 2010 are nearly double those from 1970. This contradicts economic developments, as industry has produced a declining share of the global gross domestic product (GDP). The majority of these GHG emissions (21%) are direct emissions (Scope 1), which comprised direct energy-related CO_2 emissions. Indirect emissions (accounting for 11% of industry-related GHG emissions) arose from, for example, the production of electricity and heat for industry, process CO_2 emissions and waste/wastewater emissions.

In operations management, we often look at resource use in the wider sense. Let us consider two examples here: energy and water. Industry consumes 24.2% of global energy[5] related to

DOI: 10.4324/9781003345077-5

the manufacturing of products across different industry sectors, including iron and steel, mining, food, construction, transport equipment, machinery, textiles and paper and pulp. At the same time, the production of energy is responsible for 87% of global GHG emissions.[6] Therefore, looking into industrial production and operations with the goal of improving energy efficiency and reducing the carbon intensity of energy sources has great potential for improving environmental sustainability globally.

Similarly, industry plays a strong role in the current and future use of water. Currently, industry is responsible for 12% of all water withdrawals globally (outperformed by agriculture with 72% and municipalities with 16%).[7] In much of Europe and North America, industry is the main source of water withdrawals, with the numbers ranging between 50% and 75%. Water demand is set to increase by 2050 – with estimates varying between 20% and 33%[8] – and this increase in demand is set to arise mostly from the manufacturing industry.

Many efforts are hence put into increasing the efficiency of water use. This indicator used by the UN shows the change in the ratio of the value added to the volume of water used. Water-use efficiency is defined as the value added of a given major sector divided by the volume of water used by that sector, expressed as value/volume (commonly USD/m^3). It is an economic indicator and expresses the extent to which a country's economic growth is dependent on that country's use of water resources. It therefore addresses the impact of economic growth on the use of water resources. Globally, water-use efficiency has increased. In 2018, the industrial sector had water-use efficiency equivalent to $32.2\ USD/m^3$. Compared with 2015, this represents an increase of 15% in the industrial sector.[9] Despite these achievements and continued efforts, much further work remains to be done to increase the ratio of resources used to the value provided by the output.

The usefulness of efforts to increase efficiency is limited by the amount of waste created in the system.

> Over the 20th century, the world increased its fossil fuel use by a factor of 12, whilst extracting 34 times more material resources. Today in the EU, each person consumes 16 tonnes of materials annually, of which 6 tonnes are wasted, with half going to landfill.[10]
>
> *(p. 2)*

These numbers suggest that a third of resources end up as waste. In the food sector, these numbers can be even higher. As *The Guardian* reported in 2015,

> [e]ach year 1.3bn tonnes of food, about a third of all that is produced, is wasted, including about 45% of all fruit and vegetables, 35% of fish and seafood, 30% of cereals, 20% of dairy products and 20% of meat.[11]

While the redirection of waste from landfills into value streams is something that is discussed again in Part III, here, we will look at how to avoid the creation of waste in the first place.

Despite the focus of this section on environmental measures of resource use and efficiency, measures also cover the economic and social sustainability pillars. Example measures to assess sustainability in operations management are shown in Table II.1. These measures can help identify suitable goals for implementing sustainable operations management in an organisation. However, targeted sustainability-related efforts are required to achieve these goals.

TABLE II.1 Example measures for assessing product sustainability[a]

Economic	Environment	Social
Operation cost	Emissions: CO_2, greenhouse gases (GHGs)	Health and safety: noise level, number of near misses, percentage of accident-free workstations, percentage of workstations with high noise levels, recordable incident rate and number of fatal accidents
Demand: economic order quantity and number of back orders	Consumption: water, energy (energy efficiency), hazardous/ harmful/toxic materials and degree of water reuse	Employment: employee satisfaction
Delivery lead time		Labour productivity
Taxes, tax breaks		Employee training and development
Process costs		Employee participation: number of employees' suggested improvements
Supplemental indicators: costs attributable to fines and penalties, environmental responsibility costs and number of claims for worker compensation	Waste generated	Turnover rate or average length of service of employees
	Recycling, reduction of waste	Labour conditions, including low wages, working hours, exploitation of employees and rights to form unions
	Environmental policies and audits; environmental costs, magnitude and penalties for non-compliance	Child labour
Customer response time, order cycle time and order fulfilment lead time		Human rights
		Minority development
	Effects on biodiversity	Inclusion of disabled or marginalised people
		Gender equality

a Based on, for example, Allaoui, H., Guo, Y., Sarkis, J. (2019). Decision support for collaboration planning in sustainable supply chains. *Journal of Cleaner Production*, vol. 229, pp. 761–774. https://doi.org/10.1016/j.jclepro.2019.04.367; Ahi, P., Searcy, C. (2015). An analysis of metrics used to measure performance in green and sustainable supply chains. *Journal of Cleaner Production*, vol. 86, pp. 360–377. https://doi.org/10.1016/j.jclepro.2014.08.005; Yawar, S.A., Seuring, S. (2017). Management of social issues in supply chains: A literature review exploring social issues, actions and performance outcomes. *Journal of Business Ethics*, vol. 141, pp. 621–643. https://doi.org/10.1007/s10551-015-2719-9; Tajbakhsh, A., Hassini, E. (2015). Performance measurement of sustainable supply chains: A review and research questions. *The International Journal of Productivity and Performance Management*, vol. 64, pp. 744–783. https://doi.org/10.1108/IJPPM-03-2013-0056

Part II of this book looks at the role of operations management in reducing resource use. This can and needs to be achieved by addressing and increasing the resource efficiency of industry. "The World Business Council for Sustainable Development estimates that by 2050 we will need a 4 to 10 fold increase in resource efficiency, with significant improvements needed already by 2020."[12] Resource efficiency plays a crucial part in achieving sustainable development goals. "[Resource efficiency] allows the economy to create more with less, delivering greater value with less input, using resources in a sustainable way and minimising their impacts on the environment."[13] How to achieve resource efficiency is a central question in operations management.

Technology can play an essential part in achieving this aim and increasing resource efficiency – see, for example, the Box "Quote: Mitigation of climate change." However, other approaches are available and need to be explored. For example, the European Commission writes: "Improving the re-use of raw materials through greater 'industrial symbiosis' (where the waste of some firms is used as a resource for others) across the EU could save €1.4bn a year and generate €1.6bn in sales."[14] The Commission refers to the potential effects of resource efficiency in the German manufacturing industry, where a study estimated potential cost savings of 20%–30% and up to 1 million additional jobs. It also refers to the potential effects in the United Kingdom, where £23 billion in savings could be generated through increasing resource efficiency.

Quote: Mitigation of climate change

The energy intensity of the sector could be reduced by approximately up to 25% compared to current levels through widescale upgrading, replacement and deployment of best available technologies, particularly in countries where these are not in practice and for non-energy intensive industries (robust evidence, high agreement). Despite long-standing attention to energy efficiency in industry, many options for improved energy efficiency remain. Through innovation, additional reductions of approximately up to 20% in energy intensity may potentially be realized before approaching technological limits in some energy-intensive industries...

Besides sector-specific technologies, cross-cutting technologies and measures applicable in both large energy-intensive industries and small and medium enterprises (SMEs) can help to reduce GHG emissions (robust evidence, high agreement). Cross-cutting technologies such as efficient motors, electronic control systems, and cross-cutting measures such as reducing air or steam leaks help to optimize performance of industrial processes and improve plant efficiency cost-effectively with both energy savings and emissions benefits...

Mitigation measures in the industry sector are often associated with co-benefits (robust evidence, high agreement). Co-benefits of mitigation measures could drive industrial decisions and policy choices. They include enhanced competitiveness through cost reductions, new business opportunities, better environmental compliance, health benefits through better local air and water quality and better work conditions, and reduced waste, all of which provide multiple indirect private and social benefits.

Source: IPCC (2014). Climate Change 2014: Mitigation of Climate Change. Contribution of Working Group III to the Fifth Assessment Report of the Intergovernmental Panel on Climate Change [Edenhofer, O., R. Pichs-Madruga, Y. Sokona, E. Farahani, S. Kadner, K. Seyboth, A. Adler, I. Baum, S. Brunner, P. Eickemeier, B. Kriemann, J. Savolainen, S. Schlömer, C. von Stechow, T. Zwickel and J.C. Minx (Eds.)]. Cambridge University Press, Cambridge, United Kingdom and New York, NY, USA.

In short, the potential to increase sustainability performance across the triple bottom line exists, and it is significant. Operations management, with its focus on resource use and transformation, plays a crucial role in increasing this performance. The potential to achieve these benefits is explored in this part.

Notes

1   Slack, N., Brandon-Jones, A. (2019). *Operations Management*, 9th ed., Pearson Education Limited.

2 European Commission. (2011). Roadmap to a resource efficient Europe. Communication from the Commission to the European Parliament, the Council, the European Economic and Social Committee and the Committee of the Regions, EU COM 571, available from: https://ec.europa.eu/environment/resource_efficiency/about/roadmap/index_en.htm; p. 2.

3 IPCC (2014) Climate Change 2014: Mitigation of Climate Change. Contribution of Working Group III to the Fifth Assessment Report of the Intergovernmental Panel on Climate Change [Edenhofer, O., R. Pichs-Madruga, Y. Sokona, E. Farahani, S. Kadner, K. Seyboth, A. Adler, I. Baum, S. Brunner, P. Eickemeier, B. Kriemann, J. Savolainen, S. Schlömer, C. von Stechow, T. Zwickel and J.C. Minx (Eds.)]. Cambridge University Press, Cambridge, United Kingdom and New York, NY, USA. pp. 743–744.

4 The majority of this CO_2eq measure is indeed CO_2 with 85.1%. This is followed by CH_4 (8.6%), HFC (3.5%), N_2O (2.0%), PFC (0.5%) and SF6 (0.4%) emissions.

5 Based on ourworldindata.org, accessed in October 2021.

6 Based on ourworldindata.org, accessed in October 2021.

7 https://www.unwater.org/publications/summary-progress-update-2021-sdg-6-water-and-sanitation-for-all/

8 Burek, P., Satoh, Y., Fischer. G., Kahil, M.T., Scherzer, A., Tramberend, S., Nava, L.F., Wada, Y., Eisner, S., Flörke, M., Hanasaki, N., Magnuszewski, P., Cosgrove, B., Wiberg, D. (2016). Water Futures and Solution Fast Track Initiative – Final Report published by International Institute for Applied Systems Analysis.

9 FAO and UN Water. 2021. Progress on change in water-use efficiency. Global status and acceleration needs for SDG indicator 6.4.1, 2021. Rome. https://doi.org/10.4060/cb6413en. These results were produced using data available from 166 countries for 2015–2018 and can provide an overall picture of the change in water-use efficiency globally.

10 European Commission. (2011). Roadmap to a resource efficient Europe. Communication from the Commission to the European Parliament, the Council, the European Economic and Social Committee and the Committee of the Regions, EU COM 571, available from: https://ec.europa.eu/environment/resource_efficiency/about/roadmap/index_en.htm; p. 2.

11 https://www.theguardian.com/environment/ng-interactive/2015/aug/12/produced-but-never-eaten-a-visual-guide-to-food-waste

12 European Commission. (2011). Roadmap to a resource efficient Europe. Communication from the Commission to the European Parliament, the Council, the European Economic and Social Committee and the Committee of the Regions, EU COM 571, available from: https://ec.europa.eu/environment/resource_efficiency/about/roadmap/index_en.htm; p. 2.

13 European Commission. (2011). Roadmap to a resource efficient Europe. Communication from the Commission to the European Parliament, the Council, the European Economic and Social Committee and the Committee of the Regions, EU COM 571, available from: https://ec.europa.eu/environment/resource_efficiency/about/roadmap/index_en.htm; p. 3.

14 European Commission. (2011). Roadmap to a resource efficient Europe. Communication from the Commission to the European Parliament, the Council, the European Economic and Social Committee and the Committee of the Regions, EU COM 571, available from: https://ec.europa.eu/environment/resource_efficiency/about/roadmap/index_en.htm; p. 6.

3

SUSTAINABLE PRODUCTION

One of the most important resources across industry sectors is energy. As described in the introduction to Part II, industry uses much of the energy currently produced and will require an even larger portion of global energy production in the future. Conversely, industry is also one of the sectors where the most impactful effects can be achieved through resource efficiency.

Consider the life-cycle assessment (LCA) about shopping bags described in Chapter 2. One of the contributors to the environmental impact of the shopping bags under comparison was production, and energy use was a central factor here. The Box "Tool: LCA of shopping bags – Energy use during production" shows the part of the LCA that focuses on the production phase of the shopping bags. Before delving into the details of this chapter, try "Exercise: Examples of organisations improving their energy use."

Tool: LCA of shopping bags – Energy use during production

The UK Environment Agency carried out an LCA of commonly used shopping bags. They compared the following four bags: a lightweight carrier made from high-density polyethylene (HDPE), a "bag for life" made from low-density polyethylene (LDPE), a heavier plastic bag with stiffening inserts made from non-woven polypropylene (PP) and a cotton bag. As part of their study, the analysts estimated the CO_2-equivalent emissions from the production of these four types of bags. In addition to the material flows, the study also traced all energy flows into and out of the system. The primary determinant of the energy flows was the production of the various bag options.

To estimate the environmental impacts created through production, the analysts had to collect specific data and make different kinds of assumptions. Based on their research, they found that all plastic bags were produced from plastic melt, which was processed in different ways depending on the specific bag. In general, the plastic melt was blown and sealed. However, for the non-woven PP bag, a spun-bonded process was used. The necessary energy was typically provided through the grid. The analysts

DOI: 10.4324/9781003345077-6

were able to measure the energy consumption and waste generated for the production of 1,000 bags, as shown in Table 3.I.

TABLE 3.I Energy consumption and waste from producing 1,000 bags

Bag type	Electricity	Heat (from natural gas)	Heat (from heavy fuel oil)	Waste
HDPE bag	6.151 kWh (0.758 kWh/kg)			418.4 g
Bag for life (LDPE)	32.58 kWh (0.932 kWh/kg)	13.953 kWh (0.399 kWh/kg)		171.2 g
PP bag			87.75 kWh (0.758 kWh/kg)	5,850 g
Cotton bag	11 kWh (0.06 kWh/kg)			1,800 g

The analysts estimated that 90% of LDPE bags were produced in Turkey and Germany with the remaining 10% produced in China and Malaysia. The HDPE bags were imported from China. Producers provided the relevant data to estimate the LCA for these bags. The country of production was used to estimate the GHG emissions from energy production which is typical in these countries. Regarding waste, the analysts posited that the waste generated through the production of HDPE, LDPE and PP bags was recycled (which was confirmed by the bag producers). As the analysts were not able to receive any direct data from producers of cotton bag, some assumptions were necessary. They assumed that cotton bags were produced in China with electric sewing machines. The production waste was assumed to go to landfills. The production of paper bags was analysed in a prior publication; the analysts used these data for their estimations.

Based on these assumptions and data, the analysts calculated the emissions from the production of the shopping bags. The emissions refer to the number of shopping bags needed to carry 483 items (the average UK monthly shop). These numbers differ by type of carrier bag, depending on the volume of each individual bag and consumer behaviour in packing items into them (see more detail in Chapter 2). The environmental impact of each type of shopping bag is listed in Table 3.II. Note that these values are estimated based on the reported total global warming potential and relative contribution from the production phase, as the report did not detail absolute values based on each life-cycle phase.

TABLE 3.II

Bag type	Global warming potential across life cycle [kg CO_2 eq]
HDPE bag	0.443
Bag for life (LDPE)	1.502
PP bag	1.900
Cotton bag	0.417

Source: Edwards, C., Fry, J.M. (2011). Life cycle assessment of supermarket carrier bags: A review of the bags available in 2006. Bristol, UK. https://assets. publishing.service.gov.uk/government/uploads/system/uploads/attachment_ data/file/291023/scho0711buan-e-e.pdf

> ### Exercise: Examples of organisations improving their energy use
>
> What examples from industry can you think of in which organisations attempted to improve their energy use? What did they do?

(Sustainability) performance

Operations performance has traditionally been assessed in terms of effectiveness and efficiency based on the following definitions of these terms:

Effectiveness can be defined as successfully achieving a pre-defined outcome.

Efficiency is defined as achieving a pre-defined outcome with the lowest possible use of resources, including material, time and energy.

An effective operation is one in which the value proposition a company offers is delivered upon, meeting a customer need. An efficient operation delivers this output through the lowest possible use of resources, which in turn reduces the cost of producing the product or service. An efficient operation can only be achieved when effectiveness is established. Use the "Exercise: Elevator" to apply the two terms.[1]

> ### Exercise: Elevator
>
> Think of the operations of an elevator, transporting a person from Floor A (where they are on at the moment) to Floor B (where they would like to be). What makes this operation effective? What makes it efficient?

Based on the basic definitions above, the terms "eco-efficiency" and "eco-effectiveness" can be defined. Recall the definitions from Chapter 2; for simplification, we repeat them here as follows:

Eco-efficiency is achieved by delivering competitively priced goods and services which satisfy human needs and improve quality of life while progressively reducing ecological impact and resource intensity throughout the life cycle to a level at least in line with the earth's estimated carrying capacity.

Eco-effectiveness refers to beneficial environmental, social and economic traits of goods and services.

Eco-effectiveness and eco-efficiency are not conceptually linked. Eco-efficiency essentially means that existing outputs are continuously produced while a company tries to reduce the amount of (and type of) resources used in the process. Most current industry examples where companies aim to reduce their environmental impact are examples of eco-efficiency. Eco-efficiency initiatives aim for the "low hanging fruit" to achieve meaningful effects with a relatively low amount of investment and effort. These efforts can also target non-core operations, as detailed in the Box "Example: Siemens." However, most of these initiatives are based on a linear logic of the traditional cradle-to-gate or cradle-to-grave approaches (see Chapter 2). One of the resulting problems with eco-efficiency is the potential rebound effect: More efficient production can actually lead to higher consumption, meaning that no noteworthy positive net effects are achieved.

Example – Siemens

In 2006, Siemens initiated a process for improving internal energy efficiency across its global network of facilities, including offices and production plants. The process consisted of four steps:

1 Select site for improvement.
2 Perform an energy health check.
3 Analyse the energy use.
4 Implement performance improvement contract between the facility and corporate HQ.

This process resulted, among other impacts, in the installation of energy-efficient equipment and processes worth 1.9 million Euros in a plant in Bavaria, Germany. Through this installation, Siemens reduced the use of energy in the plant by 20%, cut emissions by 2,700 metric tonnes of CO_2 and produced annual savings of 700,000 Euros. This example illustrates how performance across two of the sustainability pillars (planet and profit) can be well aligned. The savings must be compared to the 2,737,000 metric tonnes of CO_2 emissions that Siemens produced in 2013. In light of this figure, Siemens created savings of 0.1% of its emissions through one factory.

Other initiatives implemented by Siemens through this process included extension of existing building automation, modernisation of measurement and control technology for heating and installation of energy-efficient lighting. Initiatives like these at 298 production plants worldwide improved energy efficiency by 11% and CO_2 efficiency by 20% between 2010 and 2014.

Source: Sheffi, Y., Blanco, E. (2018). *Balancing Green: When to Embrace Sustainability in a Business (and When Not To)*. MIT, Chapter 4; https://www.publics. bg/en/news/8600/Siemens_Energy_Costs_Reduced_by_Half_a_Million_Euros.html

---

Eco-effectiveness goes beyond eco-efficiency and proposes the transformation of products and their production processes such that they form a supportive relationship with ecological systems and future economic growth. Eco-effectiveness is often pursued through a cradle-to-cradle model, generating a cyclical approach to the material flows.

Industrial symbiosis

A frequently used and simple method of representing operations management is the input-transformation-output model (Chapter 1). Production requires different inputs (e.g., energy, heating and material), and through various processes, outputs are produced, consisting of the main products to be sold on the market and waste products. Many production processes involve either heating or cooling of ingredients, intermediate products, or finished goods or maintaining the right temperature for the industrial processes.

Many of the processes duplicate efforts – one system consumes energy to cool down hot materials, while another consumes energy to warm cold materials. This duplication offers various opportunities to generate efficiency effects.

These opportunities, however, only emerge if we take a systems view of production. If each of these production processes – one requiring heating, the other requiring cooling – is analysed individually, symbiotic effects between them are not evident. Depending on where the boundaries of the system are drawn (e.g., two production processes, a whole plant, two manufacturing plants and a whole geographic region), different symbiotic effects can be identified and savings achieved. The European Commission assesses that greater "industrial symbiosis" could save €1.4 billion a year and generate €1.6 billion in sales.[2]

Industrial symbiosis (IS) aims to make industry more sustainable by achieving collective benefit. These benefits are based on using waste, by-products and excess utilities between economically independent industries. Industrial symbiosis is based on the idea of industrial ecosystems by establishing symbiotic relationships between economically independent industries, typically in a geographically close set-up. Sustainable performance is achieved through reduced natural resource consumption and waste disposal and reduction of emissions to air, water and soil from the production of the saved raw materials (environmental) and access to cheaper sourcing, avoiding disposal costs and/or gaining extra profit from selling the by-products (economic). From a social perspective, IS emphasises the local community and increases the drive towards working cooperatively to contribute to regional economic development. As such, the ideas behind IS extend into all three dimensions of sustainability.[3]

One example is *cogeneration*, through which electricity generation and heat-dependent manufacturing systems are intentionally collocated to reduce systemic waste of energy through combining heat and power production. In combined heat and power (CHP) production facilities, the excess heat during power production is supplied to manufacturing processes instead of being wasted through release into the environment. The waste from one process (here, heat) is used as an input into another process (manufacturing), and as a result, the waste in the overall system is reduced. CHP production facilities offer some of the most efficient energy production, with efficiency rates of more than 90%. For this reason, the Danish Energy Agency uses CHP to supply more than 60% of all heat consumed in Danish households. The district heating system enables the use of excess heat that would otherwise be wasted. A further example of cogeneration is described in the Box "Example – Cogeneration: Unilever."

Example – Cogeneration: Unilever

Unilever – the globally operating producer of consumer products such as food, personal hygiene products, pet food and cleaning products – invested 28 million Euros into establishing cogeneration on its existing plant in Indiana, USA. Unilever contracted Grastim Energy to supply electricity, heat, cooling and compressed air until 2026. The Unilever Hammond Indiana plant has been in operation since 1929 and produces synthetic bar soaps for the Dove and Caress brands to supply the North American market. The plant's output is about 950 million bars of soap a year.

Under this new agreement, Grastim installed a CHP system, which runs on natural gas. The system was commissioned in 2019 and has been operational since June 2019. It is expected that cogeneration will offer over 46% greater efficiency in comparison to using a standard power plant. Through recovering the thermal energy in the engine and exhaust system, cogeneration at the Unilever Hammond Indiana plant is expected to deliver more than 90% efficiency. Unilever expects to avoid 60,000 tonnes of CO_2 emissions and to save about 10 million Euros per year through this investment. A further advantage is that the system can run in isolation if the plant experiences a power outage from the utility.

Source: https://www.clarke-energy.com/2020/unilever-hammond-indiana

The logic of cogeneration can be extended to production processes more generally. Unwanted outputs from one (sub)process can be used as inputs in another (sub)process, thereby reducing the amount of waste in the system as a whole. This ***integrated production*** system offers obvious efficiency potential. Integrated production requires consideration of the broader production system to integrate the different input resources and generated outputs to leverage co-dependencies and waste streams (see Figure 3.1). One example of such integrated production is described in the Box "Example – Integrated production: *Verbund* at BASF."

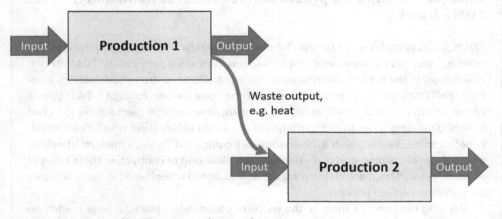

FIGURE 3.1 Integrated production, such as used in cogeneration.

Example – Integrated production: *Verbund* at BASF

BASF – the globally operating producer of chemicals and chemical products – uses integrated production to produce about 50% of its global production volume. It has established six integrated production sites globally – which they call *Verbund* – in Ludwigshafen (Germany), Antwerp (Belgium), Nanjing (China), Kuantan (Malaysia), Geismar (USA) and Freeport (USA). In these *Verbund* sites, BASF operates site-wide management of products and by-products, including wastewater, steam and electricity. Apart from achieving resource efficiency, this approach also minimises logistics and material handling. BASF uses pipelines to transport some of the resources across their *Verbund* sites, replacing time-intensive and costly filling and transport via truck, rail or ship. For example, the Ludwigshafen site integrates 160 production facilities interconnected by 2,750 km of pipelines in a 10 km^2 campus. Through this set-up, BASF saves more than 300 million Euros annually. In addition, they estimate their 2019 savings at 12.4 million MWh of fossil fuels and 2.5 million metric tonnes of CO_2.

Source: https://www.basf.com/global/en/investors/calendar-and-publications/
factbook.html

The logic of integrated production can be further extended in the context of social sustainability. Instead of viewing production as a stream of materials and resource flows, production systems can also integrate with the broader social environment, providing employment opportunities and often products for local consumers. The Box "Example – Integrated production for social sustainability: TOMS" describes one such example in more detail.

Example – Integrated production for social sustainability: TOMS Shoes

TOMS Shoes provides social benefits by placing its production sites within the communities to which they donate rather than using usual apparel supply chains. TOMS Shoes, which designs and markets shoes to consumers globally, has a strong sustainability identity. The TOMS business model is based on the "one-for-one concept." Each time a consumer buys a pair of TOMS shoes, the company gives another pair of shoes to a child in need. Donating shoes to children who cannot afford to buy them offers direct health benefits. Some diseases, such as hookworm, are contracted through the feet; therefore, giving shoes to children drastically reduces their likelihood of contracting these types of diseases. In addition, many children are not able to attend school without shoes, as shoes are part of the school uniform.

Shipping the donated shoes to the recipient communities placed a large burden on TOMS' logistics system, as they needed to deliver small batches of shoes to the communities in need. Until 2014, TOMS produced all of its shoes in Asia. By 2017, 40% of the shoes they donated were made in the recipient countries, including Haiti, Kenya, India, Ethiopia and Mexico. Through this approach, TOMS creates jobs in these communities, raises the overall wealth of people living there and thus contributes to long-term sustainability. This approach also decreases costs in the delivery time and carbon footprint of shipping shoes around the world.

Source: Lefko, M. (2017). *Global Sustainability: 21 Leading CEOs Show How to Do Well by Doing Good.* Morgan James Publishing, New York, US; https://www.forbes.com/sites/davidhessekiel/2021/04/28/the-rise-and-fall-of-the-buy-one-give-one-model-at-toms/?sh=292acb2171c4

Performance assessment and measurement

To examine if the implemented approaches and concepts achieve the desired effects, performance must be assessed and measured. Depending on the focus of the measures and analysis, different conclusions as to the performance can be drawn. See the Box "Example – Performance assessment: Apple" for an example on contradicting conclusions depending on the focus of assessment. Performance assessment is important to understand the behaviours and activities that help in achieving the goals of sustainability. Many employees value sustainability, and many organisations have sustainability initiatives driven by employees or employee groups. However, specific initiatives may not attract the wide support they need to be successful or may spark different behaviours than intended. The Box "Exercise: You get what you measure" offers some examples. Individuals often make choices to advance their own personal aspirations, which may not align with the original purpose of a sustainability initiative.

Example – Performance assessment: Apple

In two separate analyses about Apple's activities and corporate investments, the two non-for-profit organisations Greenpeace and Truthout came to contradicting conclusions. Reviewing Apple's annual report in 2015, Greenpeace and Truthout each identified different potential performance effects of the company's investments and activities.

Greenpeace highlighted that Apple was spending $848 million over 25 years to purchase solar power as well as $1.8 billion to construct and operate two data centres in Ireland and Denmark to provide renewably powered Apple data in Europe. Greenpeace further highlighted the partnership with SunPower to build solar plants in China to use and invest in renewable energy in Apple facilities. Apple's goal was to reach 100% renewable energy, and through existing investments, Apple avoided 750,000 tonnes of CO_2 emissions from 2011 to 2015. Greenpeace hence gave Apple a "thumbs up" for their sustainability efforts.

Truthout, in contrast, came to the conclusion that Apple's efforts were insufficient. They noted that Apple facilities accounted for just 1% of the company's CO_2 emissions in 2014. In fact, Apple's emissions had increased, which was not just due to an increase in sales but also due to a huge increase in manufacturing and transportation emissions per unit sold. Thus, production of Apple's products was actually growing progressively dirtier in terms of emissions – not cleaner and not greener. The average life-cycle emissions increased 41% from 69.1 kg of CO_2 per product sold in 2010 to 92.9 kg of CO_2 per product sold in 2014. Apple's MacBook series is the worst offender, with 262.1 kg of CO_2 emitted per product sold. Based on this assessment, Truthout gave Apple a "thumbs down," though they did praise Apple for their transparency on emissions.

Source: Sheffi, Y., Blanco, E. (2018). *Balancing Green: When to Embrace Sustainability in a Business (and When Not To)*. MIT Press, Cambridge, Massachusetts, USA, Chapter 4.

Exercise: You get what you measure

What behaviours might the following performance assessment criteria spark?

1   A production manager at a steel mill receives a production bonus based on tonnes produced.
2   A salesperson receives commission based on value of sales.
3   A maintenance team is assessed by speed of repairs performed.
4   A call-centre operator must average 20 calls an hour.

Source: Gardiner, D., Reefke, H. (2020). *Operations Management for Business Excellence: Building Sustainable Supply Chains.* Routledge, Abingdon, UK, p. 209.

One issue when defining sustainability initiatives is the time frame: Sustainability-related initiatives often need long-term time frames to achieve the intended effects. In contrast, business evaluations often focus on short-term effects measured quarterly or annually. Thus, time frames and incentives often have to be mixed together to assess sustainability-related effects in conjunction with other factors, such as cost savings.

Hoshin kanri

One approach to identify meaningful criteria to assess performance is hoshin kanri. Hoshin kanri offers a systematic process for defining long-term aims in organisations and translating them into mid- and short-term objectives throughout the organisational hierarchy. The term translates from Japanese to "policy management" and defines the process for a top-down approach for defining aims and objectives with bottom-up reviews for performance assessment. Figure 3.2 depicts the logic of hoshin kanri.

The top-down approach for defining aims and objectives is based on the following process:

1   The organisation's vision is determined by top management. This vision defines the long-term strategy, including achieving or targeting specific sustainability-related goals.

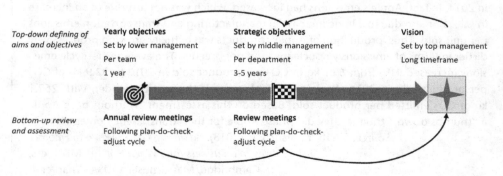

FIGURE 3.2   Process of hoshin kanri.

2 The vision is translated by middle management or team experts into strategic objectives. Strategic objectives detail goals according to time frames of three to five years and can look differently for different departments of the organisation.
3 The strategic objectives, in turn, are translated into yearly objectives on the team level. These yearly objectives cover a time frame of one year and apply to specific teams.

The hoshin kanri process can be extended to define monthly, weekly or even daily objectives. This process can also be applied to define individual-level objectives (see, for example, the Box "Exercise: Hoshin kanri for personal goals"). Each step is taken in concession. When one management level completes the task of setting objectives, they pass down the task to the next level within the organisation, prompting the lower level to add their inputs and interpret the high-level objectives as they affect them. This cascading process is a vital step in hoshin kanri aimed at empowering the organisation to generate buy-in at every level, resulting in ownership across the organisational hierarchy.

Exercise: Hoshin kanri for personal goals

Imagine yourself ten years from now – how do you want your life to look? Where would you like to work and live? Define a vision for the long-term goals in your life.

Now try to break this vision down into strategic objectives. What do you need to achieve in the next three to five years to stay on track for accomplishing this vision? Is there anything you need to do in addition to completing your university degree to achieve your vision?

Finally, break these strategic objectives down into yearly objectives. What do you need to achieve in the coming year to stay on track for achieving your strategic objectives?

Hosin kanri also consists of a bottom-up review cycle, which starts from the lowest-level objectives. Reviews are conducted annually and can also be incorporated into monthly and weekly operations. Reviews follow the plan-do-check-adjust cycle: Progress is measured against the target set at the beginning of the year (plan). Actual results are written alongside each objective (do), and any difference between the target and the actual achievements is noted (check). Finally, the impact of the results is documented, potentially leading to adjustments in performance.

Reviews result in an analysis of objectives – whether they were achieved or not – to identify what went right and wrong. The purpose is to determine if the supporting strategies and performance measures are appropriate. The underlying premise is one of learning, to identify how to do better and to transfer that knowledge across the hierarchical levels in the organisation. The aim is to learn from non-performance, not to attribute blame or hide responsibility from higher-level management. This process will position the organisation for improved performance in the future and allows it to be adaptive and self-healing. As such, hoshin kanri allows performance assessment across different time frames by aligning short-term actions with long-term goals.

Environmental and social profit and loss

There are various industry initiatives that try to capture the performance assessment of sustainability investments. In a first step, the focus is on an environmental profit & loss (E P&L) account. An E P&L measures the environmental footprint and then calculates the monetary value of this footprint.[4] This approach was first imagined by Kering Group, a group of luxury brands including Gucci, Saint Laurent and Alexander McQueen. An E P&L allows companies to achieve the following:

- To understand where impacts are.
- To develop knowledgeable decision-making processes.
- To responsibly steer business strategy.
- To strengthen the business and manage risks for the future.
- To be transparent with stakeholders.

Kering was the first group to release a complete E P&L for each of their 20 brands. Together with other companies (e.g., Natura – Brazil, Unilever) led by the World Business Council for Sustainable Development (WBCSD), Kering is creating an international protocol for the E P&L, the "natural capital protocol," and is also measuring social impacts in a social P&L.

Solutions

Example: Elevator

In the case of an elevator, effectiveness is safely moving the waiting person from Floor A to Floor B. An effective operation is established when the value proposition is delivered: when the person arrives (safely) on Floor B.

Efficiency relates to the time it takes the person to get from Floor A to B. This duration includes waiting time, travel time and potential stops on other floors to pick up or drop off other people. The result is contradicting demands on the operation. For example, an efficient operation in relation to a single user would reduce his or her individual waiting time. In contrast, an efficient operation from the provider side aims to reduce the average waiting time for all users, which may in fact increase the waiting time for an individual user.

Example: You get what you measure

1 This incentive system encourages the production manager to produce fast, easy-to-make and heavy products that may not sell or will only sell at a discount. It might increase waste production and overproduction. This incentive also focuses on individual rewards, ignoring team benefits and team building practices.
2 This incentive may create capacity problems during production, as it is related to price rather than customer needs.
3 This incentive may cause the maintenance team to carry a truckload of spare parts to avoid travelling back to pick up relevant spare parts or material. It may also result in poor quality maintenance and poor customer interaction.
4 This incentive may lead a call centre operator to terminate calls at three minutes. When this behaviour is evident, a customer will call back to complete the conversation and use another three minutes. This pattern creates a higher workload in the system but results in poor customer service.

Notes

1 Some notes on answering this exercise are provided at the end of this chapter.
2 European Commission. (2011). Roadmap to a resource efficient Europe. Communication from the Commission to the European Parliament, the Council, the European Economic and Social Committee and the Committee of the Regions, EU COM 571, available from: https://ec.europa.eu/environment/resource_efficiency/about/roadmap/index_en.htm; p. 6.
3 Herczeg, G., Akkerman, R., Hauschild, M.Z. (2018). Supply chain collaboration in industrial symbiosis networks. *Journal of Cleaner Production*, vol. 171, pp. 1058–1067. https://doi.org/10.1016/j.jclepro.2017.10.046
4 https://www.kering.com/en/sustainability/measuring-our-impact/our-ep-l/what-is-an-ep-l/

4

LEAN MANAGEMENT

Lean management refers to a set of practices and tools aimed at improving the manufacturing processes of goods and the provision of services. Applying lean management can be intrinsically linked to resource efficiency, reducing the amount of waste generated in operations and hence positively impacting sustainability. However, a recent research study found that many organisations fail to sustain these benefits over time.[1] Before looking at the connections between lean management and sustainability performance, we first examine the basics of lean management.

Principles of lean management

Lean management is a process that includes five principles aimed at improving efficiency in operations and reducing waste. Figure 4.1 shows an overview of the five principles. Lean management starts with identifying the value activities provided by asking this question: Which activities in the process of manufacturing and delivering a product create value for the customer? Value-adding activities are differentiated from non-value-adding activities. Value-adding activities are those production activities a customer is willing to pay for. This includes, for example, a transformation phase during the production process, such as the cutting of a layer of cloth to produce a garment. In contrast, non-value-adding activities define those activities a customer is not willing to pay for because these activities make no change to the product. These are the causes of many kinds of waste, such as the use of resources for unproductive purposes and the lengthening of manufacturing and delivery times.

Mapping these activities in a value stream allows for identifying value-adding activities and eliminating non-value-adding activities. Value-stream mapping is a visualisation exercise to provide a vision of the future state. It enables managers to see value streams and continuously improve them. The exercise starts with the future-state map and works backwards to the current-state map; the analysis looks at the requirement to attain the future state. The future state encompasses the ideal customer and employee experience; it should

DOI: 10.4324/9781003345077-7

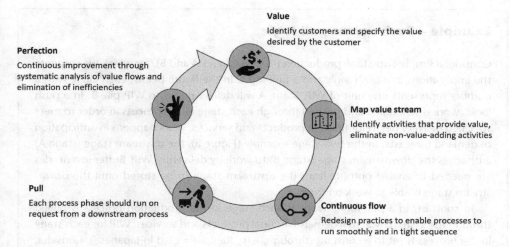

Value
Identify customers and specify the value desired by the customer

Perfection
Continuous improvement through systematic analysis of value flows and elimination of inefficiencies

Map value stream
Identify activities that provide value, eliminate non-value-adding activities

Pull
Each process phase should run on request from a downstream process

Continuous flow
Redesign practices to enable processes to run smoothly and in tight sequence

FIGURE 4.1 Five principles of lean management. Based on Gardiner, D., Reefke, H. (2020). *Operations Management for Business Excellence: Building Sustainable Supply Chains.* Routledge.

be the perfect process. With the perfect process as the ideal, the question of whether each step is valuable, capable, available, adequate and flexible is asked. In this way, a value-stream map enables the differentiation of value-adding and non-value-adding activities and the elimination of the latter from the production process. Good maps are action statements and highlight where the organisation can target improvement steps.

Once the non-value-adding activities are eliminated, flow is created by ensuring that the production system functions without interruptions. Interruptions can be caused by different circumstances, such as unexpected downtimes from machine breakdowns or the unavailability of materials due to supply delays. These interruptions cause inefficiencies in the production system and waste through wait times and the excessive accumulation of work in progress (WIP). It is hence necessary to identify and implement practices and solutions that enable processes to run smoothly and in tight sequence.

Once the processes have been redesigned to create flow, pull logic is applied to ensure that each phase of the process step is carried out only when a specific request was made by the downstream process step. For the end product, this order is initiated by the final customer, who can be external. As a result, nothing is produced (neither finished nor semi-finished products) if demand for it has not been indicated – based on just-in-time (JIT) production. The Box "Example – Push versus pull logic" shows how pull logic can create efficiencies in a production system. This reduces inventory and, as a result, removes variability in the production system hidden by inventory. This variability is reduced through solving problems in the system that the inventory serves to hide. This is based on the assumption that inventories are created to patch the symptoms instead of solving the problem. However, in practice, these problems may be outside of the control of an organisation. Current industry practices indicate that JIT production can be problematic for production systems – see the Box "Note: Auto makers retreat from 50 years of 'just-in-time' manufacturing."

Example – Push versus pull logic

Consider a simple two-stage production process (stages A and B), for which we compare the implications of a push logic and a pull logic. In the figure below, each circle with a number represents one unit of WIP. Stage A will deliver unit 6 to WIP pile B. In a push logic, work is scheduled and pushed through each stage in the process in order to meet specified delivery needs for finished products and services. Work happens in anticipation of demand forecasts. In the two-stage example (Figure a), the upstream stage (stage A) authorises the downstream stage (stage B) to work by delivering WIP. Buffer inventories are needed to enable outputs from the upstream stage to be stored until the downstream stage is able to work on them.

In contrast, in a pull logic, work at each stage in the production process is pulled through the system by actual demand for final products and services. WIP for each stage in the process is set to a constant (through, e.g., Kanban = card in Japanese). Consider, for example, a set value at stage B of four units – this means that the maximum WIP waiting to start processing at stage B is four units, similar to buffer inventory B. If stage A completes its work on unit 6, it will only deliver that unit to WIP pile B when stage B completes work on unit 1. At that time, unit 6 is delivered to WIP pile B, and stage A can continue working. The downstream stage (stage B) authorises the upstream stage (stage A) to work through a WIP. Ideally, no buffers are needed through a constant exchange of information or orders from the downstream stage to upstream, which authorises the delivery of WIP downstream (Figure b).

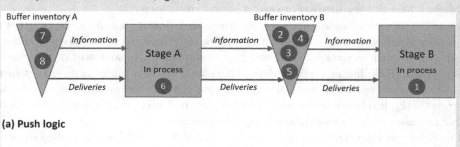

(a) Push logic

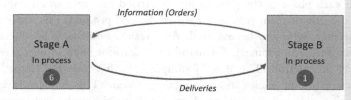

(b) Pull logic

Source: Souza, G.C. (2017). *Sustainable Operations and Closed Loop Supply Chains*, 2nd ed., Business Expert Press, New York, NY, USA

Note: Auto makers retreat from 50 years of "just-in-time" manufacturing

In May 2021, the *Wall Street Journal* reported that manufacturers in the automotive industry are retreating from JIT production. After decades of maturing supply chains and buyer–supplier relationships in this industry sector, where lean management was developed and matured, JIT principles prove impractical to the global operating conditions created in part by the coronavirus pandemic. Most notably, Toyota Motor Corp. is reported to be stockpiling parts again. The unexpected extent and unprecedented scale of the coronavirus pandemic exposed the fragility of the JIT-based supply chain model. This constitutes one of the biggest transformations of the industry sector in decades and may cause a paradigm shift in lean management.

Source: www.wsj.com/amp/articles/auto-makers-retreat-from-50-years-of-just-in-time-manufacturing-11620051251

The final principle focuses on the perfection of the redesigned system through continuous improvement. Value flows are analysed systematically and inefficiencies eliminated. This typically requires a high degree of participation from employees, who typically possess the operational knowledge of the production system required to identify opportunities for continuous improvement. Through continuous improvement, performance benefits can be achieved, as seen in the Box "Example – Pacific Seafood."

Example – Pacific Seafood

Through continuous improvement to their work processes, Pacific Seafood is now able to double the protein return from animals. This has led to reducing the environmental impact of their fishing activity by 50% with no loss in the amount of food produced. The company is dedicated to providing the healthiest protein on the planet through fish and seafood-based meals. Pacific Seafood manages all parts of the supply chain, from harvesting and fishing to the processing and distribution of the final product. Some of the company's most popular items include oysters, crab, rockfish, cold-water shrimp, wild salmon and steelhead. They assess the value their products provide through plate protein needs. The main issues in their production process are related to recovery (i.e., how much fish needs to be caught to obtain a certain amount of final product). Through continuous improvement, the company implemented new cooking and harvesting techniques. Through continuous improvement of their harvesting processes based on an in-depth understanding of biology, Pacific Seafood now achieves a 15% better recovery of oysters. Many of the sustainability initiatives come from employees due to fair treatment and an open ear from leadership. The different continuous-improvement initiatives in sum mean that the company is now able to provide the same protein value on the plate by gathering only half the amount of fish and seafood.

Source: https://www.pacificseafood.com/; Lefko, M. (2017). *Global Sustainability: 21 Leading CEOs Show How to Do Well by Doing Good.* Morgan James Publishing, New York, NY, USA.

The role of waste

One of the central objectives of lean management is the elimination of waste. This offers probably the closest and most direct connection between lean management and sustainability – covering all three pillars of sustainability defined in Chapter 1. In lean management, waste refers to all the improper uses of company resources that do not generate value for the customer. Waste can have the following causes[2]:

- *Overproduction*: Products or parts which are produced in excess quantity or too early constitute overproduction. If production volumes are not aligned with actual market demands, too much of a product or product part may be produced. Often, it is problematic to reuse overproduced products or product parts later due to, for example, obsolescence – both physically and commercially. Think of, for example, perishable products in a supermarket or the fashion industry (known as fast fashion). Even if a product or product part can be reused, it needs to be stored in a warehouse as inventory, which creates waste in the form of space or energy.
- *Excess inventory*: While inventory is traditionally seen as problematic in lean management, excess inventory is particularly wasteful because the stored product or product parts are not or cannot be used because there is no demand for them. This is often especially the case for production based on push logic.
- *Overprocessing*: Products or product parts which have functions or performance features that customers have not requested and are not willing to pay for create waste as they require production steps beyond what is needed, including design, material and production.
- *Defects*: Products or product parts that do not comply with design requirements generate waste as they cannot fulfil a need. These often must be scrapped or reworked.
- *Waiting*: Processes characterised by queues or delays create waste. Idle people or machines create waste as they are available to work but are not used for work. This may be because of a lack of customer orders or unexpected or unplanned breakdowns. Unused capacity creates waste in the production system.
- *Unnecessary transport*: Transportation, while often necessary for the distribution and collection of products and parts,[3] does not contribute to the useful transformation of a product or product part and should hence be minimised. Unnecessary transportation can be found within the production plant or between different sites.
- *Unnecessary motion*: Unnecessary movement of production-related employees creates waste because it requires more time or effort to achieve the same output. Unnecessary motion is often created by inappropriate process design or inefficiencies.

Based on the reasons outlined above, different types of waste are generated. Table 4.1 gives an overview of the waste generated by these seven categories. This waste can be related to energy, physical waste, water, emissions, noise, land contamination and biodiversity and hence particularly affect the environmental pillar of sustainability. The social pillar of sustainability is often also impacted by different types of waste, such as noise and unnecessary motion. Reducing waste is not only part of lean management, and we have seen a few examples of waste reduction through, for example, improved product design (think of the

TABLE 4.1 Seven categories of waste

Category	Examples of waste
Overproduction	More raw materials, energy and water are consumed in making unnecessary products
	Extra products may spoil or become obsolete, requiring disposal of physical waste
	Extra-hazardous materials result in extra emissions, waste disposal, land contamination and workers' exposure to the risk of injury
	Noise deriving from the production of unnecessary products affects the local community and employees
Excess inventory	More packaging to store works in progress (WIPs)
	Waste from deterioration or damage to store (WIP)
	More energy used for heating, cooling and lighting of inventory space
	Increased land usage due to the need for bigger warehouses/factories
Overprocessing	More energy and water used to carry out unnecessary processing
	More emissions, noise and land contamination due to unnecessary processing
	More parts and raw materials used to enrich the product with unnecessary features and functions
Defects	More raw materials, energy and water consumed in making defective products
	Scraps can require disposal of physical waste
	Defective products may require reworking, which results in the same problems as overproduction
	Extra-hazardous materials embedded in defective products result in extra emissions, waste disposal, land contamination and workers' exposure to risk of injury
	Noise deriving from the production of defective products affects the local community and employees
Waiting	Potential material spoilage or component damage causes physical waste and need for disposal
	Wasted energy from heating, cooling and lighting during production downtimes
Unnecessary transportation and motion	More energy and emissions from transportation
	More packaging required to protect components during movement and transportation
	Damage and spills during transportation
	Higher risk of accidents and injuries to employees during transportation and movement

example "Design for manufacture: Nike Flyknit"). In this chapter, we focus particularly on water waste in operations as one example.

Water waste in operations

The need to reduce water waste in operations is evident in many areas around the globe characterised by water scarcity. Water scarcity can mean one of two things.[4] First, water scarcity can be related to a lack of sufficient water, which means that freshwater resources cannot meet the standard water demand in the area. Second, water scarcity can be related to a lack of safe water supplies. As the UN Department of Economic and Social Affairs states,

> Water scarcity already affects every continent. Around 1.2 billion people, or almost one-fifth of the world's population, live in areas of physical scarcity, and 500 million people are approaching this situation. Another 1.6 billion people, or almost one quarter of the world's population, face economic water shortage (where countries lack the necessary infrastructure to take water from rivers and aquifers).[5]

Water waste hence not only has clear environmental relevance but also creates relevance for the social pillar of sustainability.

Improving water-use efficiency is, therefore, a global imperative, with many efforts targeted at (i) increasing water use efficiency and (ii) decoupling water use from economic growth.[6] The UN assesses water-use efficiency as the ratio between the volumes of water used by different sectors and the gross value added of these sectors, measured in USD/m^3. This enables the monitoring of water-use efficiency across the globe. Depending on the level of economic development, volumes of water use vary greatly between different geographic regions, with Central and South Asia having the lowest water-use efficiency at about 4 USD/m^3, while Europe and North America range around 50 USD/m^3.[7]

Water-use efficiency also differs between industry sectors, varying substantially between agriculture, manufacturing and services (Figure 4.2). On average, water-use efficiency improved between 2015 and 2018 by 15%. This is where globally operating companies can play and have played an important role in sharing and implementing best practices across regions. For an example from the beverage industry, see the Box "Example – Improving water-use efficiency: AB InBev."

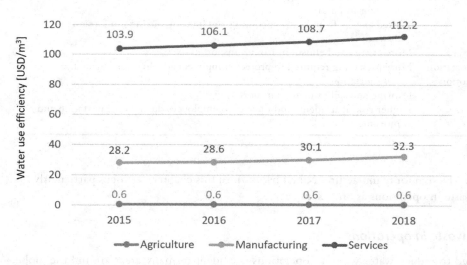

FIGURE 4.2 Change in water-use efficiency by industry sector. Based on values reported in FAO and UN Water, 2021. Progress on change in water-use efficiency. Global status and acceleration needs for SDG indicator 6.4.1. Rome, Italy. https://doi.org/ttps://doi.org/10.4060/cb641.

Example – Improving water-use efficiency: AB InBev

AB InBev, the company behind brands such as Stella Artois, made improvements to water-use efficiency in their production processes equivalent to saving 15 litres of water per litre of beer produced. They achieved this through a selection of initiatives. Similar to other producers of beverages, including Coca Cola and Nestlé, they measure and manage water efficiency as a way to improve resource efficiency in their operations and reduce waste. Many of their operations are set in "water-stressed" regions. Initially, AB InBev focused on non-product initiatives, such as controlling evaporation losses in the malting process, condensing the water stream and reusing treated wastewater for factory cleaning.

One area of high water consumption is in the raw material used for beer production. Barley growth takes about 298 litres of water per litre of beer. While beverage producers have little control over water use when growing barley, they can change the amount of barley used in their production processes. Producing beer creates extract losses, which are the fermentable sugars left over after the brewing process. Extract losses are problematic from an environmental standpoint as they dissolve in wastewater and threaten further water use in treatment plants, rivers and other areas. In addition, extract losses require the producer to buy more of the high-water-footprint grain to produce a given volume of beer. In 2002, AB InBev reported extract losses of 8%, which means they had to buy 8% more grain than the theoretical brewing efficiency limit. By analysing their global network of production plants, they were able to set clear performance targets for lagging factories and apply learnings from best-practice factories. Through this approach, AB InBev reported extract losses of only 3% in 2013. These improvements indicate the importance of the supply chain in sustainability concerns as targeting one part of the supply chain (input resources in terms of barley) may produce benefits in another part of the supply chain (production processes through brewing).

Source: Sheffi, Y., Blanco, E. (2018). *Balancing Green: When to Embrace Sustainability in a Business (and When Not To)*. MIT Press, Cambridge, Massachusetts, USA, Chapter 4; https://www.ab-inbev.com/sustainability/2025-sustainability-goals/water-stewardship/

Lean management and sustainability

The principles of lean management and the underlying philosophy aiming to reduce waste seem well aligned with principles of sustainable performance. And, indeed, recent studies investigating the connection between lean management and sustainability performance suggest alignment through a positive relationship. Various research studies have confirmed a positive relationship between implementing lean management and achieving sustainability performance across the three pillars of sustainability. Measured sustainability performance factors are listed in Table 4.2.

While earlier works have confirmed that implementing lean management has positive sustainability performance effects, more recent works have studied the extent of these effects. Specifically, recent studies have identified that how long sustainability performance can be sustained appears to be related to the maturity of implementing lean principles in the

TABLE 4.2 Sustainability performance factors achieved through implementing lean management practices[a]

Economic	Environmental	Social
Reduced production cost	Reduced air emissions	Safe working conditions for
Increased labour productivity	Reduced wastewater	operators; decreased health and
Improved profits	generation	safety incidents; fewer injuries
Reduced product development costs	Reduced solid waste	and lost days due to injuries
Decreased energy costs	Decreased consumption	Improved skill sets and boosted
Reduced inventory costs	of hazardous, harmful	employability
Reduced rejection and rework costs	and toxic materials	Team spirit and cohesiveness
Decreased raw material purchasing	Reduced energy	Trust between management and
costs	consumption	workers
Decreased waste treatment costs	Decreased frequency	Sense of accomplishment
Decreased fines for environmental	of environmental	Decreased levels of stress
accidents	accidents	Improved labour relations
	Improved environmental	Improved morale
	situation for enterprise	Decreased work pressure

a Based on: Chavez, R., Yu, W., Jajja, M.S.S., Song, Y., Nakara, W. (2020). The relationship between internal lean practices and sustainable performance: Exploring the mediating role of social performance. *Production Planning & Control*, vol. 33, pp. 1–18. https://doi.org/10.1080/09537287.2020.1839139; Hirzel, A.K., Leyer, M., Moormann, J. (2017). The role of employee empowerment in the implementation of continuous improvement: Evidence from a case study of a financial services provider. *International Journal of Operations & Production Management*, vol. 37, pp. 1563–1579. https://doi.org/10.1108/IJOPM-12-2015-0780; Kamble, S., Gunasekaran, A., Dhone, N.C. (2020). Industry 4.0 and lean manufacturing practices for sustainable organisational performance in Indian manufacturing companies. *International Journal of Production Research*, vol. 58, pp. 1319–1337. https://doi.org/10.1080/00207543.2019.1630772; Mohaghegh, M., Blasi, S., Größler, A. (2021). Dynamic capabilities linking lean practices and sustainable business performance. *Journal of Cleaner Production*, vol. 322. https://doi.org/10.1016/j.jclepro.2021.129073; Ng, R., Low, J.S.C., Song, B. (2015). Integrating and implementing Lean and Green practices based on proposition of Carbon-Value Efficiency metric. *Journal of Cleaner Production*, vol. 95, pp. 242–255. https://doi.org/10.1016/j.jclepro.2015.02.043; Piercy, N., Rich, N. (2015). The relationship between lean operations and sustainable operations. *International Journal of Operations and Production Management*. https://doi.org/10.1108/IJOPM-03-2014-0143; Yang, M.G., Hong, P., Modi, S.B. (2011). Impact of lean manufacturing and environmental management on business performance: An empirical study of manufacturing firms. *International Journal of Production Economics*, vol. 129, pp. 251–261. https://doi.org/10.1016/j.ijpe.2010.10.017; Zhu, Q., Sarkis, J. (2004). Relationships between operational practices and performance among early adopters of green supply chain management practices in Chinese manufacturing enterprises. *Journal of Operations Management*, vol. 22, pp. 265–289. https://doi.org/10.1016/j.jom.2004.01.005.

organisation. Companies can implement lean principles on different levels and to different extents within their operations and supply chains, leading to different levels of maturity of lean management in different companies. For example, Mohaghegh and co-authors found in their study different sustainability performance effects for what they call "lean adopters" in comparison to "lean duplicators."[8] Lean adopters consider "lean management not only as a thorough package but ... also sufficiently modify and develop existing practices to keep them relevant for sustainable performance" (p. 13). In contrast, lean duplicators focus on performing based on standard lean practices. Similarly, Hirzel and co-authors differentiate five levels of implementing continuous improvement practices in an organisation.[9] In sum,

TABLE 4.3 Maturity of lean implementation affecting sustainability performance[a]

Maturity level of lean implementation	Low	High
Example characteristics	Adoption of a selection of standard practices of lean management, including JIT production or total quality management	Adoption of lean management as a package of principles and practices that include softer dimensions, such as customer involvement, supplier partnership and human resource management
	Little adaptation of lean management over time	Adaptation of lean management over time as business context evolves and changes
	Management shows interest in individual employees (their tasks, difficulties, successes, etc.) and recognises changes in performance	Management has regular and open discussions with individual employees to develop a sense of workload and pressure and provide proactive support
	Problems are identified systematically	High levels of employee participation to identify and implement improvements
	Basic knowledge of customer expectations and initial thoughts on how to measure fulfilment of customer requirements	Full picture of customer requirements, which are continually measured, reported and improved with a permanent emphasis on customer feedback
Sustainability performance	Short-term outcomes and quick wins	Long-term, sustained performance outcomes

a Based on Hirzel, A.K., Leyer, M., Moormann, J. (2017). The role of employee empowerment in the implementation of continuous improvement: Evidence from a case study of a financial services provider. *International Journal of Operations & Production Management*, vol. 37, pp. 1563–1579. https://doi.org/10.1108/ IJOPM-12-2015-0780; Mohaghegh, M., Blasi, S., Größler, A. (2021). Dynamic capabilities linking lean practices and sustainable business performance. *Journal of Cleaner Production*, vol. 322. https://doi. org/10.1016/j.jclepro.2021.129073.

lean management can look fundamentally different in different organisations based on the level of maturity, as shown in Table 4.3.

In sum, the connection between lean management and sustainability performance is clear, with positive effects on all three pillars of sustainability. However, the sustained nature of this effect depends on the maturity of the organisation implementing lean management. Mature lean management implementation not only adopts standard principles but also embraces the softer elements of lean management in terms of, for example, managing closer and more transparent relationships with suppliers, embracing employee participation and involving the customer. The mature implementation of lean management hence affects supply chain management and, through that, creates better sustainability performance. This connection between supply chain management and sustainability performance is discussed in more detail in Part III.

Notes

1 Mohaghegh, M., Blasi, S., Größler, A. (2021). Dynamic capabilities linking lean practices and sustainable business performance. *Journal of Cleaner Production*, vol. 322. https://doi.org/10.1016/j.jclepro.2021.129073
2 Based on, for example, Wills, B. (2009). *Green Intentions: Creating a Green Value Stream to Compete and Win*. CRC Press, New York.
3 Transportation and sustainability will be covered in Chapter 8.
4 https://www.fao.org/land-water/water/water-scarcity/en/
5 https://www.un.org/waterforlifedecade/scarcity.shtml
6 FAO and UN Water (2021). Progress on change in water-use efficiency. Global status and acceleration needs for SDG indicator 6.4.1. Rome, Italy. https://doi.org/ttps://doi.org/10.4060/cb6413en
7 Based on FAO and UN Water (2021) Progress on change in water-use efficiency. Global status and acceleration needs for SDG indicator 6.4.1. Rome, Italy. https://doi.org/ttps://doi.org/10.4060/cb641
8 Mohaghegh, M., Blasi, S., Größler, A. (2021). Dynamic capabilities linking lean practices and sustainable business performance. *Journal of Cleaner Production*, vol. 322. https://doi.org/10.1016/j.jclepro.2021.129073
9 Hirzel, A.K., Leyer, M., Moormann, J. (2017). The role of employee empowerment in the implementation of continuous improvement: Evidence from a case study of a financial services provider. *International Journal of Operations & Production Management*, vol. 37, pp. 1563–1579.

5

SERVITIZATION

Many manufacturing firms do not only produce and sell products but also support these products during their use. In terms of the terminology introduced in Chapter 2, the operations of many manufacturers move beyond the cradle-to-gate mentality and extend into later product life–cycle phases to support the products' use and operation at the customer site. The following formal definition of servitization forms the basis for this chapter:

> Servitization describes the strategy of manufacturing firms to "offer fuller market packages or bundles of customer-focused combinations of goods, services, support, self-service, and knowledge".[1]
>
> (p. 314)

Servitization is a development observed in all industry sectors over recent decades. Manufacturers of equipment in the healthcare industry offer product support services to the same extent as companies operating in the mining, cement, automotive, and electronics industries. Large companies employ servitization as much as small and medium enterprises (SMEs).

Servitization is particularly valuable for specific types of products, namely products with long life cycles (specifically long use phases), minimal innovation (i.e., experiencing little change over time) and high value (i.e., expensive to replace). However, there are also examples of servitization for products that do not fulfil all of these characteristics.

Servitization requires that manufacturers dive into the world of services and service provision. As a strategy, it offers many possibilities for improving sustainability. However, before we delve deeper into these possibilities, we must establish the underlying terminology and connections of servitization.

Services and products

In considering different examples of services we consume in our lives – see "Exercise: What are services?" – the broad range is striking. A service can comprise anything from a discreet interaction to a longitudinal, repeated interaction. Services can serve functional purposes or entertainment purposes. So how do we define a service?

DOI: 10.4324/9781003345077-8

Exercise: What are services?

What examples of services can you name? What services do you use in your daily life?

Sampson (2010) provided a review of the history of definitions of services, which can be summarised by the three main types of definitions listed in Table 5.1. Following this review, a service can be defined as follows[2]:

> A service is an activity or a process characterised by a triangular relationship between the service provider, the customer and the service issue.

Figure 5.1 illustrates this triangular relationship. In many cases, the service issue is a product, such as maintenance services or software installation. However, it can also be the body of the customer, as in healthcare services or hairdressing. Take a moment to revisit the examples you identified in "Exercise: Services as triangular relationship."

The combination of the interaction between provider, customer and service issue is represented in the service concept. The service concept can consist of core and peripheral service elements, which include the following elements[3]:

*   *Supporting facilities:* physical and structural resources that must be in place for the service to be delivered.
*   *Facilitating goods:* materials, supplies and merchandise that are used or consumed in the service delivery process.

TABLE 5.1 Evolution of defining services

	Definition and description	*Criticism*
Binary	The service sector includes all "nonindustrial" companies. This definition traces back to nineteenth-century works and is applicable to garbage collection, healthcare and government services, among other fields	Focuses on what services are not instead of defining what they are and how they can be characterised: definition does not capture software, data manufacturing or data services
Continuum	There exists a continuum between goods (tangible-dominant) and services (intangible-dominant). In services, the output is an idea, which cannot be physically touched. Examples are advertising, designing and promoting. A good, in contrast, can be described as "a thing" which can change hands. This type of definition developed in the 1960s and 1970s	Inability to apply to service businesses that contain elements of tangibility: touching a customer or their belongings in tangible ways (e.g., such as tooth extraction and medical surgery). Similarly, computer software is intangible but is typically considered a product
Focused definition	Services are defined in terms of their own characteristics, most often, "services are products that are processes." For example, a pencil is a product (not a process), but using a pencil is a process (writing), and making a pencil is a process (manufacturing). Services provide value to a product – a pencil is only valuable if one can draw with it	Leads to the understanding that everything is a service. For example, software is a process – process that acts on data

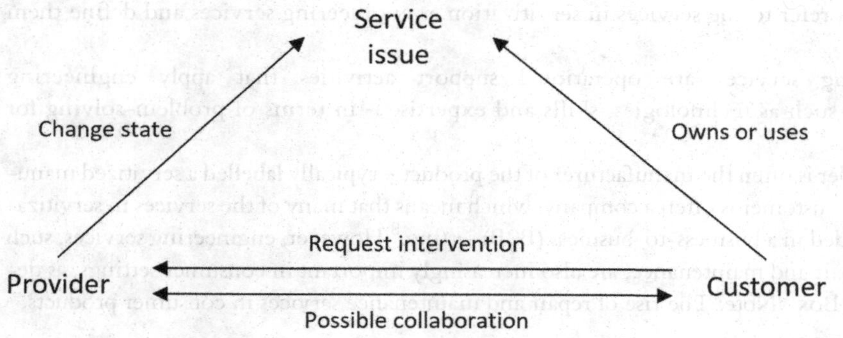

Service
issue

Change state   Owns or uses

Request intervention

Provider   Customer

Possible collaboration

FIGURE 5.1 Triangular relationship between provider, customer and service issue. Based on Araujo, L., Spring, M. (2006). Services, products, and the institutional structure of production. *Industrial Marketing Management*, vol. 35, pp. 797–805.

Exercise: Services as a triangular relationship

Revisit some of the examples you identified in the exercise: "What are services?" Try to name the provider and customer and identify the service issue.

- *Facilitating information:* information that supports or enhances the execution of the explicit services.
- *Explicit services:* customer's experiential or sensual benefits.
- *implicit services:* psychological benefits or more tacit aspects of the service that customers may sense only vaguely.

One important characteristic of services is the role of the customer. One of the key distinguishing features of a service in comparison to manufacturing is the immediacy of operations. In manufacturing, the customer becomes involved after production. A factory manufactures a home appliance and sends it to a distributor, who sends it to a retailer, who sells it to a customer, but only then starts to use or consume the product. The end customer therefore has very little input during production. In services, the customer is also a provider. The customer often owns the service issue and must make it available for the service to be provided. Thus, through service provision, we move away from the linear input-output model and towards a more circular approach.

Services in servitization

A large range of operational activities fall in the definition of services provided above. Various classifications exist based on the degree of customer interaction and customisation,[4] the nature of the service act, the level of judgment exercised by service personnel or the method of service delivery.[5]

Servitization focuses on a sub-set of services which fall under the definition provided above. In servitization, services revolve around a product, often a piece of technology such as a piece of manufacturing equipment, a pump, a plane engine, or even a whole production plant. We can refer to the services in servitization as engineering services and define them as follows[6]:

Engineering services are operational support activities that apply engineering knowledge – such as technologies, skills and expertise – in terms of problem-solving for customers.

The provider is often the manufacturer of the product – typically labelled a servitized manufacturer.[7] The customer is often a company, which means that many of the services in servitization are provided in a business-to-business (B2B) setting.[8] However, engineering services, such as product repair and maintenance, are also increasingly important in consumer settings, as described in the Box "Note: The rise of repair and maintenance services in consumer products."

Note: The rise of repair and maintenance services in consumer products

The "right to repair" is on the rise, granting consumers increasing control and the ability to maintain and repair their electronic products and thereby extend their use phase. In January 2022, the think tank of the European Parliament published a note on the European Commission's intent to establish the right to repair as a new regulation for producers. This development would allow consumers access to repair services by the manufacturer or third parties as well as self-repair support. For example, Apple announced a self-service repair programme for "customers who are comfortable" with repairing their own devices. To enable self-repair, companies need to provide easy access to original spare parts (such as screens for a mobile phone) and access to manuals and diagnostic tools. Some platforms, such as iFixit, also offer a list of third-party service providers to which consumers can bring their electronic devices for repair. The right to repair development aims to extend the life cycles of electronic devices and reduce electronic waste.

Source: https://www.europarl.europa.eu/thinktank/en/document/EPRS_ BRI(2022)698869#:~:text=The%20European%20Commission%20has%20 announced,development%20of%20a%20circular%20economy.&text=Rates%20 of%20repair%20depend%20on,important%20reason%20consumers%20 avoid%20repair; https://www.ifixit.com/Right-to-Repair/Intro; https://www. bbc.com/news/technology-57744091; https://www-bbc-co-uk.cdn.ampproject. org/c/s/www.bbc.co.uk/news/technology-59322349.amp

---

Incentives and potential for sustainability

A service-based set-up creates different incentives for a manufacturer in comparison to a product-based set-up. In a product-based set-up (or production), the manufacturer is concerned only with the production of the product and will hence optimise the production process. Such optimisation has traditionally focused on the cost of production. While this cost is connected to resource use, in a singular product, the manufacturer's profits are affected by the number of products they sell. Payment is only received on sale, which often results in a high fluctuation in income for manufacturers of products with long use phases. Performance indicators in a product-based set-up typically focus on product sales, which means that the shorter a product is in use, the more products are sold (designed obsolescence).

In a service-based set-up, the manufacturer maintains some form of responsibility for the product during use and potentially disposal. As a result, the materials, products and consumables during product maintenance become cost factors. The manufacturer is therefore incentivised to prolong the service life (use) of their products and enable the intensive use of a product to make it as cost and material efficient as possible. The manufacturer also faces incentives to improve the product use process and its maintenance, for example, through enabling customers to exchange parts more easily and quickly, use materials that last longer and reuse parts after end of life. In sum, servitization incentivises manufacturers to ensure proper use and disposal of products.

Servitization consequently offers (in theory) various incentives towards reaching sustainability goals. Consider the example of car sharing in the Box "Exercise: Sustainability effects of car sharing" to evaluate some of the potential effects of this set-up.

Exercise: Sustainability effects of car sharing

Car sharing is a service through which consumers can rent a car for short periods of time. For example, a consumer may book a car to make a specific trip. The status of the car – including parking and availability – is often managed via specific phone or computer applications (apps) by the service provider without direct interaction with the consumer. These set-ups exist in many large cities, including Copenhagen, Denmark. Through car sharing, consumers do not need to own a car anymore but can instead book one when they need it.

What sustainability impacts can car-sharing platforms have in comparison to owning a car?

Table 5.2 lists the incentives servitization creates regarding the three pillars of sustainability. To date, most research on servitization has focused on enabling manufacturers to successfully become servitized manufacturers (i.e., to develop and maintain the capabilities needed to provide services and engage in closer customer relationships). We investigate the extent to which servitization delivers on this potential for sustainability in the sub-section "Servitization and sustainability."

Types of services

Servitization is often characterised as a journey whereby a manufacturer gradually adds more and more services of increasing complexity.[9] By complexity, we mean two things. First, we talk about the complexity of the service offering itself, which emphasises the number of components included in the service offering. Second, complexity refers to the provision process in terms of the resources needed to deliver the agreed outcome, including technology, human resources and knowledge, and their interrelation within the service provision. Three distinct types of engineering can be differentiated, as presented in Table 5.3, with product-oriented services typically exhibiting the lowest levels of complexity and result-oriented services the highest.

The services listed in Table 5.3 also differ in terms of customer centricity. In a product-oriented service, the interactions between provider and customer are often of a

TABLE 5.2 Sustainability potentials of servitization[a]

Sustainability pillar	Potential offered through servitization
Environmental	*Longer product life*: Services create an incentive to avoid products or components which are thrown away unnecessarily and can extend product use
	Increase resource and energy efficiency and reduce carbon emissions: Both customers and providers have an incentive to improve resource and energy efficiency in the product use phase. For customers, this will reduce the cost of operating the product. Providers are incentivised to use materials and energy efficiently to reduce costs
	Increased recycling, remanufacturing and reuse: Providers are incentivised to avoid wasting products or components at the end of life and instead introduce them into a new life cycle through reconditioning or remanufacturing. Manufacturers have easier access to the products at the end of their life cycle, enabling them to affect end-of-life decisions. Customers' willingness to accept remanufactured products or components may be increased, offering more potential for circularity.
	Increased product usage: Providers, who retain ownership of the product, have an incentive to maximise product use (utilisation). This incentive leads them to keep the product in good working condition and enable high use intensity, which can result in more customers using the product at lower costs
	Dematerialisation: Servitization enables the provider to reduce the use of materials, energy and products, as the same number of products can meet the needs of more customers
	Freedom to design for sustainability: Manufacturers have access to information about the use phase of their products, which allows them to integrate this information during product design. If the provider also retains ownership of the product, they also have the ability to bring improved product designs to market
Economic	*Better fulfilment of customer needs*: Offerings can be customised to specific customer needs, offering tailored functionalities and improving overall value for the customer. Services are more flexible and allow the provider to respond rapidly to changing market conditions
	Customer lock-in: Customers are bound to a manufacturer through long-term service contracts, which can increase customer loyalty
	Lock out competitors: Service-based business models are more difficult to imitate, as they tend to be unique to the provider-customer dyad
	Increased revenues: Services offer a more stable and continuous revenue stream in comparison to products; profit margins can be higher
	Access to service data: Service provision offers access to product use data, including product performance and customer behaviour. This data in turn can be used to improve product design and provide insights into changing demand
Social	*Stronger customer relationships*: Service-based relationships require direct customer inputs, resulting in stronger, longer and direct customer relationships
	Increased jobs: Provision of services can create more jobs, as services are usually labour intensive

a   Based on Yang, M., Evans, S. (2019). Product-service system business model archetypes and sustainability. *Journal of Cleaner Production*, vol. 220, pp. 1156–1166, Table 1.

TABLE 5.3 Three types of engineering services in servitization[a]

	Product-oriented service	Use-oriented service	Result-oriented service
Description	Focus is on product sales, with services aimed at supporting the product use, for example, through maintenance contracts, financing schemes or supply of spare parts or consumables	Focus is on the product use. The product is made available for use by the customer in different forms	Focus is on the result (i.e., outcome of the service process), which is agreed between provider and customer. Achieving this result is independent from a pre-determined product
Examples	Installation Consultancy regarding most efficient use of product Transportation Maintenance and support	Operational lease Product renting/sharing Product pooling System health monitoring Availability contracting	Activity management Functional result Pay-per-service unit Performance-based contracts

a   Based on, for example, Tukker, A. (2004). Eight types of product-service systems: eight ways to sustainability? *Business Strategy and the Environment*, vol. 13, pp. 246–260.

transactional nature: The provider can wait until the customer raises a concern or a need for the service. For example, the provider can wait until the customer calls with a request for a new spare part or a maintenance visit to repair the product. In contrast, result-oriented services typically require intricate and close collaboration between provider and customer. To ensure that a product can deliver the agreed result, the provider often needs to know about customer operations and use patterns. For examples of the different types of engineering services, see the Boxes "Example: Product-oriented service – Siemens," "Example: Use-oriented service – Michelin" and "Example: Result-oriented service – FLSmidth."

Example: Product-oriented service – Siemens

Siemens Healthineers has incorporated customer support into their business for a long time and offer various services for their healthcare products, including magnetic resonance imaging (MRI) scanners and computerised tomography (CT) scanners. With these services, Siemens implements the philosophy that a manufacturer's role does not end with the installation of the product. They offer, for example, the following support activities to their customers:

- Quality inspections.
- Safety inspections.
- Legal inspections.
- 24h availability.
- Spare parts.
- Preventative maintenance.
- Remote service.
- Virus safety.

Source: https://www.siemens-healthineers.com/dk/products-services

Example: Use-oriented service – Michelin

Michelin – the globally operating manufacturer of tyres for cars and other vehicles – provides service guarantees. Through service packages, companies buy 100,000 miles worth of tires and receive verified low-rolling resistance tires in return. This service offering increases business for Michelin through the service fee and the incentive to use Michelin tires for replacements. The service also reduces the environmental footprint of trucking because high-quality and correctly inflated tires have longer lives and less rolling resistance, leading to lower fuel consumption and fewer tire replacements. Michelin offers the following activities:

- GoGreen initiative
- Pay by the mile
- Guarantee of working condition of tires
- Installation, maintenance, replacement, recycling

Source: https://business.michelinman.com/tips-suggestions/go-green

Example: Result-oriented service – FLSmidth

FLSmidth, the global producer of cement production equipment and plants, provides operations and maintenance (O&M) services. In long-term service arrangements, the company guarantees the output performance of their cement plants in terms of tonnage of cement produced. This guarantee means that FLSmidth operates and maintains the customer plant, which includes, for example, providing 200–300 employees to operate the plant, conducting maintenance activities, managing availability and installing spare parts, ensuring process control and ensuring health and safety standards are met on the plants. Through these O&M services, FLSmidth can also control emissions from cement production by placing filters and other controls on the equipment for improved emissions and emission control. The O&M services constitute a shift of responsibility from customer to provider, meaning that operations become a "black box" for the customer.

Source: https://www.flsmidth.com/en-gb/services

Service process

Services traditionally exhibit the following characteristics:

1 *Services are labour intensive*: This refers to the ratio of the labour costs incurred to the value of the plant and equipment. It excludes inventory.
2 *Services require high customer contact*: This refers to the relative importance of front-office and back-office operations. Front-office operations comprise the physical or virtual point where the customer interfaces directly with the service provider (usually for service

delivery) and are thus visible to the customer. In contrast, back-office operations are the part of the service operation that is completed without customer contact (e.g., billing, service planning and procurement of spare parts) and are often invisible to the customer.

3 *Services contain high levels of customisation*: Customisations are required to satisfy a particular (individual) customer need.

However, even given these characteristics, there is a spread between different service offerings. This diversity can be depicted in a service process matrix[10] which distinguishes specific services based on the degree of labour and the degree of customisation, as depicted in Figure 5.2. For services with a high degree of labour, managers typically focus extensively on human resources. This focus includes selection of qualified personnel, training service engineers (e.g., product certifications) and customer relationship management. Services with a low degree of customisation tend to have a standardised set of offerings, which restricts the choices of customers, and a high degree of automation. These services are particularly well suited for using digital technologies to support service delivery in order to improve efficiency or offer additional service support to customers.

The three characteristics of service mentioned above – labour intensiveness, high customer contact and customisation – affect the productivity of services (i.e., how efficiently service processes can be designed). The following different approaches can be implemented to increase service process productivity[11]:

- Self-service – Enabling customers to examine, compare and check out at their own pace. This approach can be particularly aided through the use of digital technology, for example, in the form of a service portal.
- ostponement – Customising the offering at delivery based on a standardised service design.
- Focus – Restricting offerings to limit customers; choices.
- Modules – Offering a modular selection of services to standardise each module and the process of delivering the service module, while enabling customers to combine modules based on their specific needs.

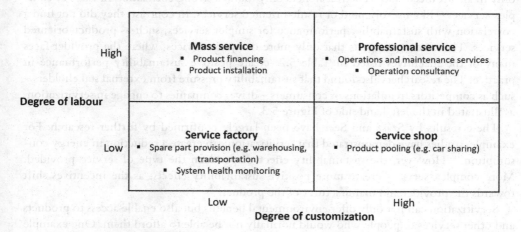

FIGURE 5.2 Service process matrix with servitization examples.

- Automation – Separating services for automation from labour-intensive services.
- Scheduling – Practising precise personnel scheduling to optimise resource availability.
- Training – Clarifying service options and explaining to the customer how to avoid problems. This approach enables the customer to self-serve.
- Separation – Structuring the service process such that the customer must go where (part of) the service is offered. For many services in the context of servitization, there are limitations to separation, as the product may be placed on a customer site, defining the location of service activities.

Servitization and sustainability

Incentive structures and product responsibility are transformed through servitization in such a way that sustainability improvements can be achieved, as summarised in Table 5.2. Servitization drives the manufacturer closer to customer operations and hence enables them to address downstream Scope 3 emissions (see Chapter 1) and thereby improve environmental sustainability. With the same incentives, servitization also enables manufacturers to reduce the cost of using their products (economic sustainability pillar). However, most servitization efforts to date have focused on establishing the capabilities needed to be a servitized manufacturer based on the specific characteristics of services, such as the service process. Emerging research has studied the sustainability effects of servitization in terms of achieving the possibilities outlined in Table 5.2. These studies suggest that servitization can indeed achieve these sustainability possibilities, depending on the type of service offered.

One previous study connecting servitization with sustainability (Szász and Seer, 2018) was based on a survey of 735 manufacturing plants from 21 countries across the globe. The researchers examined the sustainability performance of servitized firms depending on the type of service offered. The survey also questioned whether external sustainability pressures, which define the extent to which stakeholders' pressure influences company operations, drive the importance of services as a competitive priority (=servitization).

Figure 5.3 offers an overview of the connections the researchers found. According to their results, servitization positively affects an organisation's sustainability performance, but only in an advanced state. The researchers only found a strong correlation in cases of complex services – like use-oriented or result-oriented services. In contrast, they did not find a correlation with sustainability performance for simpler services, such as product-oriented services. This finding suggests that only more complex services, where the provider faces many of the incentives listed in Table 5.2, create positive sustainability performance in practice. The researchers also found that sustainability pressure from external stakeholders – such as competitors, regulations or consumers – drives companies to engage in servitization, as illustrated in the left-hand side of Figure 5.3.

These results by Szász and Seer have been largely confirmed by further research. For example, studies have demonstrated that servitization can create a reduction in energy consumption.[12] However, the sustainability effects depend on the type of service provided. More complex services create more positive sustainability effects, as the incentives shift towards the provider and manufacturer of the product.[13]

Servitization can not only offer environmental benefits but also enable access to products and other services to people who would normally not be able to afford them. One example is the pay-per-use battery-sharing model described in the Box "Example: Per-per-use – Mobile Power."

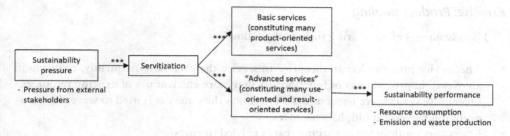

*** p<0.01 – showing a strong correlation

FIGURE 5.3   Connections between servitization and sustainability. Based on Szász, L., Seer, L. (2018). Towards an operations strategy model of servitization: The role of sustainability pressure. *Operations Management Research*, vol. 11, pp. 51–66. https://doi.org/10.1007/s12063-018-0132-0.

Example: The power of a pay-per-use battery-sharing model

Mobile Power uses a pay-per-use service model to provide smart battery packs to consumers in sub-Saharan Africa. The service-based business model allows the provider to offer the products at a price that is affordable to low-income households and avoids consumer debt. Before Mobile Power entered the market, many consumers in these countries experienced difficulties in accessing the energy they needed. Many needed to use generator-run phone-charging kiosks. Through solar-powered Mobile Power (MOPO) hubs in central locations, customers can access mobile batteries. After use, customers return the battery to the hub, where it is charged for the next customer. An installed hub has the capacity to deploy and charge 300 mobile batteries per week. The company plans to expand this business model into the e-mobility market to establish a system of pay-per-use motorbikes.

Source: https://www-esi--africa-com.cdn.ampproject.org/c/s/www.esi-africa.
com/industry-sectors/future-energy/talking-points-the-power-of-a-pay-per-use-
battery-rental-model/?amp=1; https://www.mobilepower.co/

Solutions

Exercise: What are services?

Some exemplar services are as follows:

- Medical services (e.g., doctor visits, dentist, accident and emergency – A&E, hospitals and vaccination).
- Beauty services (e.g., hairdressing).
- Entertainment services (e.g., cinemas, restaurants, cafes, ice cream parlours and sport competitions).
- Transportation (e.g., flying, car rental, car sharing services and bike rental).
- Education (e.g., universities, schools, nurseries, music lessons, art classes and sport clubs).

Exercise: Product pooling

The advantages of car sharing include the following:

- The service provider has an incentive to service the cars more frequently, resulting in an overall improved level of functionality and more efficient use of existing resources.
- Overall, fewer cars are needed in the system, as the same car is used to serve the transportation needs of multiple consumers.
- Fewer cars result in fewer parking spaces needed in cities.
- Fewer cars result in fewer road accidents.
- Car sharing can lead to higher rates of electric cars on the road, resulting in lower emissions.
- Through the payment scheme (pay per time using the car), consumers are incentivised to drive less.
- Cars used for car sharing are typically small (optimised for inner-city transport) and drive with low use of fuel (or energy).
- Providers face incentives to properly dispose of cars after their use.

Notes

1 Vandermerwe, S., Rada, J. 1988. Servitization of business: adding value by adding services. *European Management Journal*. vol. 6, no. 4, pp. 314–324.
2 Araujo, L., Spring, M. (2006). Services, products, and the institutional structure of production, *Industrial Marketing Management*, vol. 35, pp. 797–805.
3 Roth, A.V., Menor, L.J. (2003). Insights into service operations management: A research agenda. *Production and Operations Management*, vol. 12, no. 2, pp. 145–164. https://doi.org/10.1111/j.1937-5956.2003.tb00498
4 Schmenner, R.W. (1986). How can service businesses survive and prosper? *Sloan Management Review*, vol. 27, no. 3, pp. 21–32.
5 Chase, R.B., Apte, U.M. (2007). A history of research in service operations: What's the big idea? *Journal of Operations Management*, vol. 25, no. 2, pp. 375–386. https://doi.org/10.1016/j.jom.2006.11.002
6 Based on, for example, Zhang, Y., Gregory, M., Neely, A. (2016). Global engineering services: Shedding light on network capabilities. *Journal of Operations Management*, vol. 42–43, pp. 80–94. https://doi.org/10.1016/j.jom.2016.03.006; a term often used in the literature is product-service system, which describes the combination of the product and service into a seamless offering. However, given the definition of a service above, the product is already an integral part of a service through the service issue.
7 Service delivery can also be outsourced, creating triadic or even network set-ups. This practice can be particularly useful in international service set-ups.
8 Business-to-consumer (B2C) services exist in servitization, as described by Kreye, M.E., Van Donk, D.P. (2021). Exploring servitization in the Business-to-Consumer context. *International Journal of Operations & Production Management*, vol. 41, pp. 494–516: https://doi.org/10.1108/IJOPM-07-2020-0439. However, the majority of services focus on B2B settings.
9 Kreye, M.E. (2019). Does a more complex service offering increase uncertainty in operations? *International Journal of Operations and Production Management*, vol. 39, pp. 75–93. https://doi.org/10.1108/IJOPM-01-2018-0009
10 Schmenner, R.W. (1986). How can service businesses survive and prosper? *Sloan Management Review*, vol. 27, no. 3, pp. 21–32; Heizer, J., Render, B., Munson, C. (2020). *Operations Management*, 13th ed., p. 325.
11 Schmenner, R.W. (1986). How can service businesses survive and prosper? *Sloan Management Review*, vol. 27, no. 3, pp. 21–32; Heizer, J., Render, B., Munson, C. (2020). *Operations Management*, 13th ed., p. 325.
12 Doni, F., Corvino, A., Martini, S.B. (2019). Servitization and sustainability actions: Evidence from European manufacturing companies. *Journal of Environmental Management*, vol. 234, pp. 367–378.
13 Yang, M., Evans, S. (2019). Product-service system business model archetypes and sustainability. *Journal of Cleaner Production*, vol. 220, pp. 1156–1166.

CASE 2

Sustainable energy production with Burmeister & Wain Scandinavian Contractor (BWSC)

Moving from an engineering, procurement and construction (EPC) contractor delivering turn-key power plants to providing services and service-based solutions, Burmeister & Wain Scandinavian Contractor (BWSC) has set itself on a journey to improving sustainability performance in the energy sector. While green solutions are entering the market, much can be gained from existing installed technology, especially when no alternative options for energy production are locally available. After implementing many initiatives to reduce Scope 1 emissions (direct internal emissions, such as from company facilities and company vehicles), BWSC now targets Scope 3 emissions, which promise a much higher potential impact on the sector's greenhouse gas (GHG) emissions. The service business offers the ideal basis to assess the use of products and plant equipment and to identify how to decrease CO_2 emissions in this process. Through servitization, BWSC hopes to reach the low-hanging fruit of sustainability performance through a service-based operation.

Background

Energy production is one of the areas affecting sustainability performance in all industry and society sectors and is captured in the UN GHG emissions under Scope 2. In the past 50 years, global energy production needs have grown 2.5-fold. Five percent of this need is currently supplied through renewable energy sources, while 86% is met by fossil fuels. As a result, three quarters of global GHG emissions result from the burning of fossil fuels for energy, not only creating adverse environmental impacts but also negatively affecting the health of many people. Shifting energy production towards renewable sources is a powerful trend in many countries, including Denmark and other EU countries.

BWSC and sustainability

BWSC is a globally operating engineering company within the energy production sector with a traditional focus on designing, constructing, operating, maintaining, repairing,

DOI: 10.4324/9781003345077-9

upgrading and managing equipment and whole plants for energy production. Their products include diesel engine-based power plants and boiler-based plants for energy production. The company places sustainability at the core of their organisational values, with their mission being "to supply affordable and reliable power where and when it is needed."[1] The company has implemented services including spare part provision, process optimisation, product overhaul, emission measurement and operation and maintenance (O&M) of the whole plant. With a shift towards sustainability, BWSC places services more prominently at the core of their business model and embraces the potential of servitization for achieving sustainable operation. BWSC has now extended their offerings to provide life-cycle analysis of products related to services, O&M, technical advisory and engineering services and plant and boiler upgrades and conversions.

Table C2.1 summarises some of the initiatives implemented by BWSC to address Scope 1 emissions and their status. Having achieved most of the goals of these initiatives, BWSC now aims to address Scope 3 emissions.

Limitations on energy production using renewable sources

Renewable energy sources cannot necessarily meet energy demand in all places around the world. In some areas, such as small islands (e.g., Caribbean islands), it is difficult to build the necessary infrastructure, complicating the delivery of green energy solutions and the achievement of a mix of energy sources. The reasons for these difficulties may be manifold. For example, areas may be remote, with limited connectivity. They may also be frequently impacted by natural events, such as hurricanes, which regularly destroy or disrupt some of the installed base. These areas may also not be able to provide a stable supply of renewable energy sources that can meet local demand.

As a result of these factors, these remote areas may not be able to fully replace existing technology with renewable sources. Instead, sustainability efforts need to focus on the installed base, equipment and plants that have been in place for decades already and have the potential to operate in a less environmentally invasive way. These areas have traditionally

TABLE C2.1 Initiatives aimed at reducing GHG emissions at BWSC

Environmental objective	Performance indicator
Collect environmental data on internal operations	Improvements in data collection, recording of data on waste, water, electricity, gas and oil
Reduce energy consumption in BWSC head office in Denmark	5% reduction in energy consumption per employee – achieved 8.3% in 2018
	Additional 5% reduction in energy consumption per employee
Reduce paper use at BWSC head office	Reduction in paper use by 20% per employee – achieved 35% by 2018
	Additional 20% reduction in paper use per employee
Enhance the separation of waste for recycling at BWSC head office and at power plants and construction sites	Minimum of 50% of all generated waste to be separated for recycling
	10% increase in collected plastic for reuse
Promote environmental awareness internally	Minimum two internal campaigns per year

relied on solutions such as diesel-based power generation. Despite the negative public image of such "dinosaur" technology, much can be gained from the existing installed base.

Identifying areas for improving sustainability performance

The initial idea is to identify the low-hanging fruit: improvements that will be relatively easy to implement while delivering significant savings regarding the environmental impact of operating plants. Important here is the bottom-up approach to identify potential for delivering these improvements. BWSC service employees are encouraged to initiate and explore ideas based on their technical expertise. Through technical service agreements, experienced BWSC engineers are permanently stationed at a plant to operate and maintain the plant and to provide management support, technical support, supervision and employee training. In this position, they are aware of the day-to-day operations and can understand why certain outcomes are observed.

A further advantage of the service-based set-up is partnerships with external partners. Operating a service requires close and long-term relationships with customers based on mutual trust and collaboration. By procuring services, the customer also gains access to BWSC's extensive supplier network and their expertise. For example, original equipment manufacturers (OEMs) are available to liaise with customers to troubleshoot and identify technical solutions. Sustainability requires collaboration across the supply chain.

Note

1 https://www.bwsc.com/

PART III
Sustainability and supply chains

Supply chains play a central role in achieving sustainability performance. This role has been recognised by the UN and is also evident in many of the considerations described in Parts I and II of this book. To achieve a sustainable product requires contributions from supply chain partners. When an organisation implements lean to a high level of maturity, effects will be felt in the supply chain management through the relationships created with customers and suppliers. Servitization requires an inherently closer approach to customer relationships. Focusing on supply chains is a step towards achieving wider adoption of sustainability.

The following definition of supply chain management is employed in this book:

"Supply chain management encompasses the planning and management of all activities involved in sourcing and procurement, conversion, and all logistics management activities."[1]

Supply chain management links major business functions and processes within and across organisations. As such, it drives coordination of processes and activities across functions, such as marketing, sales, product design, finance and information technology. In sum, supply chain management includes "the planning, cost, or activities involved in getting fuel to the filling station, fresh foods to the store shelf, or essential medical suppliers to the hospital emergency room."[2]

Supply chain management can be further characterised as follows[3]:

- *Flow*: enabling and ensuring flows of material/physical goods, finances, services and information through logistics networks.
- *Relationships*: creation and management of internal and external relationships with channel partners, including suppliers, intermediaries, third-party service providers and customers.
- *Value*: creation of value added through efficiencies by identifying and enabling process improvements.
- *Performance*: enabling customer satisfaction in terms of delivery performance while achieving business results and outcomes.

DOI: 10.4324/9781003345077-10

Sustainable supply chain management refers to the integration of sustainability goals – economic, environmental and social – across a focal firm's supply chain processes.[4] This result is achieved by integrating sustainability considerations with key organisational business systems designed to manage the flows of material, information and finances efficiently and effectively in the supply chain to meet stakeholder requirements and improve the profitability, competitiveness and resilience of the organisation over the short and long term.[5]

The starting point for many organisations when talking about sustainable supply chain management is to identify the sustainability stakeholders. Pressures to create sustainable supply chains can derive from different sources, including new regulations and customer demands. Figure III.1 depicts some of the sources of sustainability pressure and various sustainability stakeholders of organisations. Employees may also be a meaningful source of inspiration and identification of sustainability potential, as outlined in Part II in more detail.

Legal rules or regulations are often one of the most important sources of pressure, as they create mandatory frameworks for achieving sustainability performance. For example, regulations targeted at reducing electronic waste include the extended producer responsibility (EPR) concept, the Waste Electrical and Electronic Equipment (WEEE) Directive, law on specified household appliance recycling (SHAR) (Japan) and National Solid Waste Policy (Brazil). Regulation changes often trigger the launch of sustainability initiatives

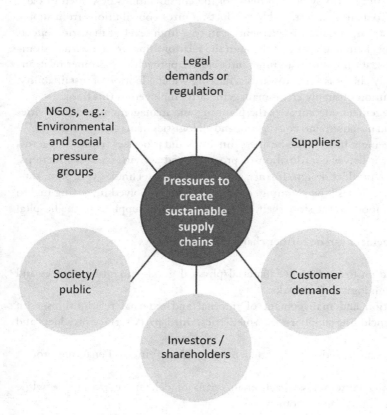

FIGURE III.1 Sources of sustainability pressure in supply chains.

in organisations or industry sectors, which are continued based on some of the following considerations.

One central source of pressure is the customer or end user of a product because these actors are the catalysts of all activities in the supply chain which determines demand. A consumer-led drive towards greener products or greener business models can initiate long-term shifts in an industry sector. On the one hand, serving this demand can create a source of competitive advantage. On the other hand, the requirements of investors and shareholders can function as a counterbalance in terms of need for (short-term) financial return and risk avoidance.

Non-governmental organisations (NGOs) can also create pressure to increase sustainability efforts in supply chains and can function as important partners, as they often conduct relevant research and maintain relevant logistics networks for communities in need. In addition, society or the broader public often serves as a relevant sustainability stakeholder. An example is described in the Box "Example – Sustainability stakeholders: Tata Group." Communication with the public is often realised through (social) media, which therefore acts as an integral sustainability stakeholder for organisations.

Example – Sustainability stakeholders: Tata Group

The Tata Group includes a broad set of stakeholders in their organisational vision to capture the broad effects of their activities:

"The Tata philosophy of management has always been, and is today more than ever, that corporate enterprises must be managed not merely in the interests of their owners, but equally in those of their employees, of the consumers of their products, of the local community and finally of the country as a whole" (1973).

The Tata Group is an Indian multinational conglomerate manufacturer of automobiles, airplanes and other products, especially in food supply chains. They include a diverse set of stakeholders within their mission statement and company vision, including "society at large" and natural ecosystems. This recognition of stakeholders is evident in their sustainability initiatives, such as their investment in the creation of a 150-acre botanical reserve for native plants and other vegetation which provides a home for threatened species (e.g., birds, tortoises and wild boar) on the site of one of Tata's soda ash facilities. A further example is the "reef recharge" project created in 2011 in collaboration with a resort and spa in the Maldives to increase fauna diversity in the area.

Source: https://www.tata.com/business/tata-sons; Lefko, M. (2017). *Global Sustainability: 21 Leading CEOs Show How to Do Well by Doing Good.* Morgan James Publishing, New York, NY, USA.

The role of supply chains in sustainability

An environmental profit and loss (E P&L) account allows companies to identify the effect of environmental sustainability initiatives (see also Chapter 3). These accounts measure the environmental footprint of an organisation and then calculate the monetary value of this footprint. Companies like Kering and Natura have pioneered E P&Ls and incorporate them into their annual reporting. Through this practice, these companies have realised that they control only a small portion of their carbon footprint – the rest is in the supply chain. Francois-Henri Pinault, Chairman and CEO of Kering, stated,

> We realize[d], for instance, that if we were to consider sustainability issues only in our legal boundaries, we would have addressed only 7% of our global carbon footprint. (…) The E P&L showed us that 93% of our carbon footprint was outside of our legal boundaries, along the supply chain in many different businesses.[6]

How upstream and downstream supply chains may or may not be outside of the legal boundaries of a focal firm is discussed more in the Box "Note: Legal responsibility."

Note: Legal responsibility

A court in the Hague has ordered Royal Dutch Shell to cut its global carbon emissions by 45% by the end of 2030 from 2019 levels. The court told Shell that they "had a duty of care and that the level of emission reductions of Shell and its suppliers and buyers should be brought into line with the Paris climate agreement." The legal case against Shell, which began in 2019, was brought by Friends of the Earth alongside six other bodies and more than 17,000 Dutch citizens. The court ruling is significant for various reasons. The verdict concluded that the Shell group is responsible for its own CO_2 emissions and those of its suppliers. This conclusion extends the legal responsibility of an organisation from the environmental sustainability-related actions of its internal operations to those of its supply chain partners as well. The case also marks the first time that a company has been legally obliged to align its policies with the Paris climate accords. Although the decision only applies in the Netherlands, it could have wider effects elsewhere.

Source: https://www.bbc.com/news/world-europe-57257982, May 2021.

Conversely, the impact that sustainable supply chain management practices can have on achieving sustainable performance targets is massive. The Box "Note: Sustainable supply chain management in the food industry" describes an example of the difficulties faced and the potential benefits created.

Note: Sustainable supply chain management in the food industry

Large companies, such as PepsiCo and Mars, increasingly recognise the potential of raw materials and packaging in reducing their carbon footprints and have called for a redesign of supply chains. Both companies have realised that about 90% of their GHG emissions are created within their supply chains. However, redesigning supply chains around sustainability is often characterised as a monumental task. Especially in the food industry, products can consist of inputs from hundreds of thousands of suppliers. Many of these suppliers are small-scale farmers, who differ in location, type of crop, size and maturity of sustainability concerns. The journey often starts with mapping the supply chain and assessing the operations of suppliers. In the case of Mars, they have assessed 20,000 raw material suppliers in more than 100 countries. The company estimates that it takes between six months and two years to map out a supplier's carbon footprint. Helping suppliers transition to more sustainable operations has also come at a high investment cost for Mars, who have invested $1 billion into achieving this goal. The potential impact is massive: If farmers changes their practice, this creates knock-on effects to their communities and their customers. Mars estimates that they have impacted around $500 billion in business through their supply chain management activities.

Source: https://finance-yahoo-com.cdn.ampproject.org/c/s/finance.
yahoo.com/amphtml/news/climate-change-mars-and-pepsi-co-
offer-lessons-in-decarbonization-calls-for-a-redesign-of-supply-
chains-170942910.html, November 2021.

One of the most visible effects of a lack of sustainability in supply chains is waste. Global waste generation is expected to grow by about 70% to 3.4 billion tonnes by 2050.[7] The European Union (EU) estimates that they produce 2.7 billion tonnes of waste annually, 98 million tonnes of which is hazardous.[8] Less than 20% of (solid municipal) waste is recycled globally every year, with 44% still going to landfills. In the EU, some member states report recycling rates as high as 80%, "indicating the possibilities of using waste as one of the EU's key resources. Improving waste management makes better use of resources and can open up new markets and jobs, as well as encourage less dependence on imports of raw materials and lower impacts on the environment."[9] Much of this waste is generated because of mismatched supply and demand, meaning that solutions lie in the management of supply chains.

However, in practice, many barriers stand in the way of achieving sustainability in supply chains. These barriers include the following[10]:

- *Communication*: Supply chain partners speak different languages and have different expectations and levels of enthusiasm for sustainability. This difference may be based on suppliers' size and extent of operations. For example, global firms often have suppliers ranging from small and specialised companies to large companies.
- *Responsibility*: It is often unclear how much responsibility a large global company has for their suppliers and their suppliers' suppliers.
- *Goal sharing and trust*: One of the strictest barriers is often the need to establish partnerships by aligning long-term strategies and ambitions across supply chain partners.
- *Regulations*: Regulations differ between countries and geographical regions, creating different needs for sustainability performance. Regulation, however, can also lead to harmonisation across supply chains in terms of expectations.

Measuring sustainability in supply chains

Supply chains have a broad range of measures for the three pillars of sustainability due to the broad nature of activities under sustainable supply chain management. Performance effects are often aligned across these pillars. For example, Wilhelm et al. reported that implementing environmental sustainability into supply chains creates an immediate link between cost reduction and quality improvements.[11] In contrast, this link is more difficult to establish between social sustainability and economic considerations.[12] Table III.1 lists some exemplar measures from the literature, which offer an idea of the nature of performance indicators and performance goals as the basis for the following chapters.

TABLE III.1 Exemplar measures for assessing product sustainability[a]

Economic	Environment	Social
Total material cost	Energy consumption, including transportation and embedded energy in used material; total energy consumption over the life cycle of a product	Health and safety: percentage of suppliers receiving safety training
Total waste costs		
Total energy cost or average costs of each energy source		Return policy efficiency
Inventory carrying costs, order fulfilment costs, out-of-date items in warehouse and reduction of cargo damage	Amount of hazardous materials used by contracted service providers	Community development and engagement
		Value fraction of investment in ethical activities
Percentage of products with take-back policy	Emissions: CO_2 produced per unit delivered	Diversity of market
Transportation network efficiency		Percentage of suppliers from local area
		Poverty deduction rate
		Service infrastructure

a   Based on, for example, Allaoui, H., Guo, Y., Sarkis, J. (2019). Decision support for collaboration planning in sustainable supply chains. *Journal of Cleaner Production*, vol. 229, pp. 761–774. https://doi.org/10.1016/j.jcle-pro.2019.04.367; Ahi, P., Searcy, C. (2015). An analysis of metrics used to measure performance in green and sustainable supply chains. *Journal of Cleaner Production*, vol. 86, pp. 360–377. https://doi.org/10.1016/j.jcle-pro.2014.08.005; Yawar, S.A., Seuring, S. (2017). Management of social issues in supply chains: A literature review exploring social issues, actions and performance outcomes. *Journal of Business Ethics*, vol. 141, pp. 621–643. https://doi.org/10.1007/s10551-015-2719-9; Tajbakhsh, A., Hassini, E. (2015). Performance measurement of sustainable supply chains: A review and research questions. *The International Journal of Productivity and Performance Management*, vol. 64, pp. 744–783. https://doi.org/10.1108/IJPPM-03-2013-0056.

Notes

1   CSCMP, 2021. *Supply Chain Management Definitions and Glossary*. Council of Supply Chain Management Professionals, available from: https://cscmp.org/CSCMP/Educate/SCM_Definitions_and_Glossary_of_Terms.aspx

2   Gibson, Brian, J., Hanna, Joe, B., Defee, C.C., Chen, H. (2014). *The Definitive Guide to Integrated Supply Chain Management*. Council of Supply Chain Management Professionals.

3   Based on, for example, Burgess, K., Singh, P., Koroglu, R. (2006). Supply chain management: A structured literature review and implications for future research. *International Journal of Operations & Production Management*, vol. 26, no. 7, pp. 703–729; Ahi, P., Searcy, C. (2013). A comparative literature analysis of definitions for green and sustainable supply chain management. *Journal of Cleaner Production*, vol. 52, pp. 329–341; Stock, J.R., Boyer, S.L. (2009). Developing a consensus

definition of supply chain management: A qualitative study. *International Journal of Physical Distribution & Logistics Management*, vol. 39, no. 8, pp. 690–711.

4 Koberg, E., Longoni, A. (2019). A systematic review of sustainable supply chain management in global supply chains. *Journal of Cleaner Production*, vol. 207, pp. 1084–1098. https://doi.org/10.1016/j.jclepro.2018.10.033

5 Ahi, P., Searcy, C. (2013). A comparative literature analysis of definitions for green and sustainable supply chain management. *Journal of Cleaner Production*, vol. 52, pp. 329–341.

6 Quoted from Lefko, M. (2017). *Global Sustainability: 21 Leading CEOs Show How to Do Well by Doing Good*. Morgan James Publishing, New York, NY, USA, p. 112.

7 https://www.statista.com/topics/4983/waste-generation-worldwide/

8 European Commission. (2011). Roadmap to a resource efficient Europe. Communication from the Commission to the European Parliament, the Council, the European Economic and Social Committee and the Committee of the Regions, EU COM 571, available from: https://ec.europa.eu/environment/resource_efficiency/about/roadmap/index_en.htm; p. 7.

9 European Commission. (2011). Roadmap to a resource efficient Europe. Communication from the Commission to the European Parliament, the Council, the European Economic and Social Committee and the Committee of the Regions, EU COM 571, available from: https://ec.europa.eu/environment/resource_efficiency/about/roadmap/index_en.htm; p. 7.

10 https://medium.com/mitsupplychain/barriers-to-sustainability-why-suppliers-are-part-of-the-problem-and-the-solution-8a9c915996ea; Dahlmann, F., Roehrich, J.K. (2019). Sustainable supply chain management and partner engagement to manage climate change information. *Business Strategy and the Environment*, vol. 28, pp. 1632–1647. https://doi.org/10.1002/bse.2392

11 Wilhelm, M.M., Blome, C., Bhakoo, V., Paulraj, A. (2016). Sustainability in multi-tier supply chains: Understanding the double agency role of the first-tier supplier. *Journal of Operations Management*, vol. 41, pp. 42–60. https://doi.org/10.1016/j.jom.2015.11.001

12 Gimenez, C., Tachizawa, E.M. (2012). Extending sustainability to suppliers: A systematic literature review. *Supply Chain Management: An International Journal*, vol. 17, pp. 531–543; Wilhelm, M.M., Blome, C., Bhakoo, V., Paulraj, A. (2016). Sustainability in multi-tier supply chains: Understanding the double agency role of the first-tier supplier. *Journal of Operations Management*, vol. 41, pp. 42–60. https://doi.org/10.1016/j.jom.2015.11.001

6

COLLABORATIVE SUPPLY CHAINS

Achieving sustainable performance requires collaboration within supply chains. At the very least, the focal organisation needs access to information. A collaborative supply chain as part of sustainable supply chain management is defined as follows:

> the voluntary integration of economic, environmental and social considerations with key interorganizational business systems designed to efficiently and effectively manage the material, information and capital flows associated with the procurement, production and distribution of products or services in order to meet stakeholder requirements and improve the profitability, competitiveness and resilience of the organisation over the short and long-term.[1]
>
> (p. 339)

A collaborative supply chain describes how a firm engages stakeholders in their supply chain for the purpose of obtaining, processing and transferring relevant climate change-related information. Collaboration in supply chains enables organisations to overcome information asymmetry and drive sustainable development.[2]

Partners in supply chains are connected through their business agreements and practices; however, the nature of these connections can differ. Table 6.1 characterises collaborative engagements in contrast to transactional ones. Collaboration defines relationships with joint initiatives that extend beyond the requirements of day-to-day operations and aim at achieving significant improvements in the long term. Collaborative supply chains base their relationships on win-win situations rather than arm's-length scenarios, which are always win-lose situations. In collaborative relationships, supply chain partners work towards mutual goals, jointly develop processes or products and share the cost of investments.

First and foremost, partners need to share a range of information, including inventory data, demand forecasts and emission data. Collaboration between supply chain partners enables information exchange, as both parties interact frequently. Exchanged information can include the full range of sustainable performance, environmental data and information

DOI: 10.4324/9781003345077-11

TABLE 6.1 Transactional and collaborative partner engagement[a]

	Transactional engagement	Collaborative engagement
Purpose/ predominant focus	Cost-driven, aimed at identifying and implementing efficiencies Risk management	Shared value-driven Innovation and joint strategic development
Timeframe	Short to medium term	Long term
Resource sharing	Typical set-ups include the following: • No resource sharing • Operational resource sharing, including communications between operational levels, sharing operational information such as point-of-sale (POS) data	Typical set-ups include the following: • Tactical resource sharing, including communication between managers in the same function from different firms to achieve consistency or jointly developing inventory and production plans • Strategic resource sharing, such as forming strategic alliances, forming strategic-level meetings, jointly creating strategic plans, sharing strategic information or jointly investing resources to make strategic advances, especially in the area of research and development (R&D)
Benefits	Reduced inventory, reduced operating costs, increased profits, better use of resources, improved customer satisfaction and increased efficiency	Shorter lead time, improved quality, higher profit, enhanced reputation with customer satisfaction, waste reduction, compliance with laws, increased recycling, improved community health and safety, better working conditions, ability and willingness to help (donation and resource) and supply chain resilience

a Based on Allaoui, H., Guo, Y., Sarkis, J. (2019). Decision support for collaboration planning in sustainable supply chains. *Journal of Cleaner Production*, vol. 229, pp. 761–774. https://doi.org/10.1016/j.jclepro.2019.04.367; Dahlmann, F., Roehrich, J.K. (2019). Sustainable supply chain management and partner engagement to manage climate change information. *Business Strategy and the Environment*, vol. 28, pp. 1632–1647. https://doi.org/10.1002/bse.2392; Gibson, B.J., Hanna, Joe, B., Defee, C.C., Chen, H. (2014). The definitive guide to integrated supply chain management. *Council of Supply Chain Management Professionals*. Kumar, G., Subramanian, N., Maria Arputham, R. (2018). Missing link between sustainability collaborative strategy and supply chain performance: Role of dynamic capability. *International Journal of Production Economics*, vol. 203, pp. 96–109. https://doi.org/10.1016/j.ijpe.2018.05.031.

regarding social practices. Approaches to gather or exchange information between partners include the following[3]:

• *Formal and structured approaches*: structured surveys and customer data platforms (CDP); supplier audits, supplier screening and pre-contract information; formal feedback routines and suggestion schemes; benchmarking exercises; industry initiatives and industry surveys; reporting of information based on regulations; codes of conduct defined in contract terms and conditions and awards and prizes for well-performing suppliers and partners.

- *Informal and ad hoc approaches*: collaborative information exchange, inter-personal dialogue between supplier and customer contact points, voluntary sharing of practices and results of sustainability studies; supplier workshops and training and reactive responding to customer requests for information.
- *Sustainability events*: business summits with customers, suppliers and/or other supply chain partners.

Collaboration is necessary to achieve sustainable supply chains. See, for example, the Box "Note: Complexity of supply chains forces collaboration" for more detail. Efforts to create collaborative supply chains often need to extend beyond first-tier suppliers, as the most serious environmental and social breaches frequently arise from sub-suppliers. The effects of a lack of collaboration are manifold. For example, the toy producer Mattel needed to recall some of their toys in 2007 because they were coated with a toxic paint, the source of which was traced to a subcontractor of Mattel. A further example is offered by Inditex, Zara's parent company, which was charged on 52 accounts for unsustainable working conditions at one subcontractor site. The argument was that, as a clothes maker, Zara needs to know who produces their garments and is responsible for knowing about working practices in their supplier's and sub-suppliers' plants.[4]

Note: Complexity of supply chains forces collaboration

Targets of net zero and sustainability in supply chains require companies to collaborate closely. To be able to account for the greenhouse gas (GHG) emissions in their supply chains, organisations also must collaborate with their direct competitors. Such cooperation would have been unthinkable not so long ago. As internal emissions constitute only a small percentage of GHG emissions for many organisations, they need to address the emissions in their supply chains or the Scope 3 emissions. For example, the suppliers of Swiss pharmaceutical company Novartis account for 90% of the company's total Scope 3 emissions; at US telecom company Verizon, this rate is 80%.

The complexity of supply chains means that they are difficult to visualise or map. Many companies face a decentralised supplier base, often with thousands of suppliers located in hundreds of countries around the globe. Most of these suppliers also provide products and services to other companies, creating a highly interconnected global supply network.

Source: *The Financial Times*. https://amp.ft.com/content/dd06cc6c-e1ea-421a-a05e-16ed4a4a9dd0, 1st November 2021.

Supply chains without collaboration

Traditional supply chains are often characterised based on the nature of demand – stable or fluctuating. If demand is stable, supply chains tend to be designed with efficiency in mind. An efficient supply chain focuses on minimising the costs of shipping a product from the factory to the customer. In contrast, when demand is unstable or unpredictable, supply chain management focuses on responsiveness. Responsive supply chains focus on customer availability and responsive service.

In each of these settings, supply chain management is characterised by local optimisation, whereby individual organisations within the chain focus on maximising local profit or minimising immediate costs. In cases of stable demand, optimal reordering amounts and frequencies can be determined based on a stable decrease in inventory. Efforts at local optimisation, however, often result in the *bullwhip effect*. The bullwhip effect refers to large oscillations of inventory in the supply chain network caused by small changes in downstream demand, which increase in magnitude as they "travel" upstream. If end-users, for example, increase the demand for a certain item, the retailer will order this item from their wholesaler or distributor, who in turn orders from the item manufacturer, who in turn orders parts or materials from their suppliers and so on. In each step, the focal firm (e.g., retailer, wholesaler and manufacturer) places the order based on their increased demand. In general, the order size continuously increases as the demand increase travels upstream and thereby amplifies the true demand.

The bullwhip effect is one example of ill-aligned supply based on incorrect information about demand. It is a symptom of information distortion about what is really happening in the supply chain because each supply chain partner focuses on the information available in their local part of the chain. Information distortions about demand can result from the following:

- *Incentive schemes*: Incentives are designed to push products into the chain for sales that have not occurred yet and hence over-state true demand. Examples include sales incentives (e.g., the option to purchase products after collection of points for reduced prices), quantity discounts and quotas. These incentive schemes typically differ from country to country (see Box "Exercise: Incentive schemes"). Incentive schemes generate fluctuations in demand that are ultimately expensive for all members in the chain.
- *Large lots*: Many retailers tend towards buying large lots to reduce unit costs incurred, for example, on transport. However, large lots increase holding costs and fail to reflect actual demand for a product.

Exercise: Incentive schemes

What examples of incentives schemes can you think of? How do they affect buying behaviour? Do you have any personal experience with an incentive scheme?

Such initiatives create information distortions about what is really happening in the supply chain and thereby create misalignment between supply and demand. Synchronising the supply chain reduces these effects. Synchronisation and collaboration enable sharing of accurate information on demand to provide different supply chain partners' insights about how many products are actually pulled through the chain. Inaccurate information is often an unintentional side effect of marketing initiatives or cost reduction and results in distortions and fluctuations.

Collaboration in supply chains

Achieving sustainable performance effects with collaborative supply chains (Table 6.1) depends on the implementation of collaboration within the supply chain. For example, Kumar et al. found that the profile of collaboration determines the extent to which performance effects are achieved.[5] Misaligned collaboration (i.e., when the ideal profile of collaboration is not implemented) reduces the extent to which performance effects can be achieved. Scholten and Schilder (2015) similarly concluded that collaborative supply chains not only deliver sustainable performance effects but also lead to resilient supply chains. Resiliency here refers to the ability to sense and respond effectively to different incidents and crises. An example of close collaboration to secure supply is given in the Box "Example – Water supply by Carlsberg."

Example – Water supply by Carlsberg

To secure access to safe water in high-risk areas, Carlsberg collaborates with Desolinator to install water purification systems and ensure access to safe and clean drinking water for communities. The system uses solar energy for desalination, enabling transformation of sea and other water sources. With the effects of climate change affecting water supply in many regions through flooding or desertification, access to safe drinking water is an area of increasing importance. Desolinator advocates that the technology to solve the problem of access to safe drinking water exists but needs to be deployed and installed through collaborative means.

Source: https://www.weforum.org/videos/20832-carlsberg-group-announces-innovative-partnership-to-protect-shared-water-resources-in-india-uplink-yt; Carlsberg Sustainability Report 2020. https://www.carlsberggroup.com/media/42556/carlsberg-sustainability-report-2020_final.pdf

---

Truly collaborative supply chains are often difficult to achieve. Table 6.2 lists some of the advantages of and hurdles to collaboration in supply chains.

Collaborative supply chains are multidimensional, as different choices and characteristics regarding structure, relational capital and cognitive capital determine the nature and degree of collaboration within the supply chain.[6]

Structure – Supply chain configurations

Supply chain configuration can determine the extent to which different sustainability performance effects can be achieved across the three pillars – economic, environmental and social. Success depends on the extent to which these performance outcomes can be affected by the focal company directly or indirectly through working with their multi-tier suppliers. For example, environmental outcomes are often traceable and can be observed in the end product through the used material. In contrast, social outcomes are often more difficult to trace and may require stronger connection to the sub-suppliers. As a result, different supply chain configurations enable different sustainability performance outcomes.

Relevant supply chain configurations can be closed, open or based on third-party involvement, as listed in Table 6.3. Closed configurations are characterised by direct engagement

TABLE 6.2 Advantages of and hurdles to collaboration in supply chains[a]

Advantages of collaboration	Hurdles to collaboration
• Greater flow of information across the supply chain	• Need for resource allocation to supply chain management often coincides with higher costs. Ineffective allocation of resources, poorly designed processes and unrealistic time limits waste time, creating time constraints that require too much effort to manage. The need for resource allocation to supply chain management becomes a heavy burden on smaller organisations and reinforces the need to choose partners carefully
• Reduced inventory at all linkages in the supply chain	
• Effective use of resources and subsequent reduction of costs	
• Reduced lead times driven by accurate demand data	
• Increased speed to market and responsiveness	
• Service-level gains (delivery in full, on time and in specification)	
• Trained and educated purchasing employees and suppliers can function to support collaboration	• Greater coordination effort and complexity
	• Need to change old mindsets based on confrontation
• Encouragement of transparency	• Missing or incorrect communication in the supply chain, including the use of non-standardised formats for communication
• Supporting effects of monitoring, evaluation, reporting and sanctions	
• Ability to identify and evaluate potential complementarities	• Significant legal, strategic and operational barriers in terms of engaging supply chain partners in collective climate change responses
• Lower transaction costs – employment of informal relationship governance over formal to create long-term, trusting relationships	• Free-rider behaviour
	• Information can be a source of competitive advantage – free sharing may undermine this
	• Property rights – risk of imitation
• Increased supply chain resilience to disruption risks	• Information leakages to rivals

a Based on, for example, Dahlmann, F., Roehrich, J.K. (2019). Sustainable supply chain management and partner engagement to manage climate change information. *Business Strategy and the Environment*, vol. 28, pp. 1632–1647; Seuring, S., Müller, M. (2008). From a literature review to a conceptual framework for sustainable supply chain management. *Journal of Cleaner Production*, vol. 16, pp. 1699–1710.

between the focal organisation and its sub-suppliers (second-tier suppliers) and tend to exist in stable supply chains. While this structure is work-intensive for the focal firm, it enables the firm to manage sub-suppliers' social responsibility practices, which are otherwise hard to trace and often require on-site verification.

Open supply chains are characterised by a linear flow of products and information, with no direct interaction between the focal organisation and sub-suppliers. They tend to exist in supply chains with a high rate of supplier turnover. Open configurations are useful when a firm has few tier suppliers which have relatively strong sustainability capabilities. In these structures, the focal organisation engages only the first-tier suppliers in sustainability efforts and may delegate managing sustainability efforts with further sub-suppliers to these first-tier suppliers. Open configurations are particularly appropriate for achieving environmental sustainability performance because compliance can often be easily traced. In contrast, they are reported to be less effective for social sustainability concerns and for considering sustainability performance in multiple dimensions.

TABLE 6.3 Supply chain configurations[a]

	Closed supply chain configurations	Open supply chain configurations	Third-party configurations
What?	Direct engagement between focal organisation and sub-suppliers, often with formal and informal relationship governance	Linear flow of products and information with no direct interactions between focal organisation and sub-suppliers	Management of sustainability performance outcomes is (partly) outsourced to third-party organisations, such as NGOs or governments.
	[Diagram: Focal firm ↔ 1st-tier supplier ↔ 2nd-tier supplier]	*[Diagram: 2nd-tier supplier → 1st-tier supplier → Focal firm]*	*[Diagram: 3rd party (e.g. NGO), 1st-tier supplier, 2nd-tier supplier, Focal firm interconnected]*
Advantages	Ability to manage sub-suppliers' sustainability outcomes, especially with regard to social responsibility	Ability to manage outcomes in environmental dimension of sustainability because supplier non-compliance can be traced in the product Ability to manage outcomes in economic dimension	Effective for jointly achieving sustainability performance outcomes on multiple dimensions (economic, environmental and social) Typically used when focal firm has large number of suppliers
Disadvantages	Require relatively stable supply chains to build relationships with sub-suppliers	Inability to trace (non-)compliance with social sustainability performance, requires first-tier suppliers' involvement in managing sub-supplier performance Less effective for achieving sustainability performance in multiple pillars	Require interaction with multiple stakeholders Require close relationship to non-traditional supply chain partners

a Based on Koberg, E., Longoni, A. (2019). A systematic review of sustainable supply chain management in global supply chains. *Journal of Cleaner Production*, vol. 207, pp. 1084–1098. https://doi.org/10.1016/j.jclepro.2018.10.033; Wilhelm, M., Blome, C., Wieck, E., Xiao, C.Y. (2016). Implementing sustainability in multi-tier supply chains: Strategies and contingencies in managing sub-suppliers. *International Journal of Production Economics*, vol. 182, pp. 196–212. https://doi.org/10.1016/j.ijpe.2016.08.006.

Third-party configurations are characterised by the presence of non-traditional supply chain actors, such as non-governmental organisations (NGOs), governmental partners or even competitors. Here, the focal organisation may either delegate or collaborate with third-party actors for managing upstream sustainability performance outcomes. This supply chain configuration has been reported to be effective for jointly achieving sustainability performance across different pillars (economic, environmental and social).

Relational capital

Relational capital defines interaction closeness, trust, respect, friendship and reciprocity. Relational capital offers an added source for governing inter-organisational relationships beyond contractual means by offering a "softer" approach to managing regular interactions and engagements. Close collaborative relationships can be characterised through the following factors[7]:

- *Information sharing* defines the extent to which a firm shares a variety of relevant, accurate, complete and confidential information in a timely manner with its supply chain partners. This aspect is at the heart of supply chain collaboration (see also Table 6.1). Close relationships are characterised by the willingness to make strategic and tactical data such as inventory levels, forecasts, sales promotions and marketing strategies available to firms.
- *Goal congruence* between supply chain partners is the extent to which supply chain partners perceive that their own objectives are satisfied by accomplishing the supply chain objectives. It is the degree of goal agreement among supply chain partners. In the case of true goal congruence, supply chain partners either feel that their objectives fully coincide with those of the supply chain or, in case of disparity, believe that their goals can be achieved as a direct result of working toward the objectives of the supply chain. Integration enables goal alignment of supply chain partners through incentives designed to enhance supply chain performance.
- *Decision synchronisation* defines the process by which supply chain partners orchestrate decisions in supply chain planning and operations that optimise the supply chain benefits. Planning decisions are required to determine the most efficient and effective way to use the firm's resources to achieve a specific set of objectives. There are seven key supply chain management planning decision categories: operations strategy planning, demand management, production planning and scheduling, procurement, promise delivery, balancing change and distribution management. Joint planning is used to align collaborative partners and to make operating decisions, including inventory replenishment, order placement and order delivery.
- *Incentive alignment* defines the process of sharing costs, risks and benefits among supply chain partners. It includes determining costs, risks and benefits as well as formulating incentive schemes. Successful supply chain partnerships require that each participant shares gains and losses equitably and that the outcomes of the collaboration are quantifiably beneficial to all. Incentive alignment requires careful definition of mechanisms that share gains equitably, which means that gains are commensurate with investment and risk.
- *Resource sharing* defines the process of leveraging capabilities and assets and investing in capabilities and assets with supply chain partners. Resources include physical resources, such as manufacturing equipment, facility and technology.

- *Collaborative communication* is the contact and message transmission process among supply chain partners in terms of frequency, direction, mode and influence strategy. Open, frequent, balanced, two-way, multilevel communication is generally an indication of close interorganisational relationships. A "collaborative communication strategy" emphasises key communication attributes including frequency, extent of bi-directional flows, informal modes and indirect content.
- *Joint knowledge creation* defines the extent to which supply chain partners develop a better understanding of and response to the market and competitive environment by working together. There are two kinds of knowledge-creation activities: knowledge exploration (i.e., searching for and acquiring new and relevant knowledge) and knowledge exploitation (i.e., assimilating and applying relevant knowledge). The capture, exchange and assimilation of knowledge (e.g., process, technology or market knowledge) between supply chain partners enable innovation and the long-term competitiveness of the supply chain as a whole.

Cognitive capital

Cognitive capital defines the shared representations, interpretations, meanings, values, goals and understanding in the buyer-supplier relationship. It is embodied in shared codes and language and shared narrative. Shared codes and language represent goals, key performance indicators, task ownership, standardisation, training and tacit understanding, and often depend on the industry sector. Shared narratives in turn reflect past responses to issues and represent shared corporate culture, company values, philosophies, business approaches and capabilities and management styles. These may depend on national cultures. Cognitive capital is often developed via participative and continuous sense-making processes. Cognitive capital is linked to the ability to achieve sustainability performance outcomes.[8]

Extending supply chains

Collaborative efforts often result in extending supply chains by adding new supply chain partners (such as in the third-party configuration) and introducing new relationships. One example is industrial symbiosis, introduced in Part II as an operational set-up whereby waste, by-products and excess utilities are used between otherwise independent industries. The set-up often involves close geographic proximity, for example, in industrial parks. Industrial symbiosis often introduces new supply chain relationships as companies in otherwise independent industries form a new collaborative supply chain network. The traded by-products are typically outside of the core business of the supplier. Industrial symbiosis requires shared strategic vision and collective decision-making between the participating companies and necessitates mutual recognition, trust and information sharing. One example of industrial symbiosis is described in the Box "Example – Kalundborg, Denmark," which describes the connections created between an array of otherwise independent supply chains.

Collaboration can also form new partnerships when companies collaborate with the purpose of innovation and developing new products. To make existing products and their packaging more sustainable often requires collaboration with new partners, who have capabilities that are not needed in the current supply chain set-up. One such example is described in the Box "Example – L'Oréal." This case is an example of a new supply chain evolving for achieving the goal of sustainability.

Example – Kalundborg, Denmark

One inspiration and model for industrial symbiosis is the eco-industrial park at Kalundborg in Denmark, developed in 1972. The primary partners of this set-up were originally an oil refinery, power station, gypsum board facility, pharmaceutical plant and the City of Kalundborg. Since its creation, the set-up has expanded to include new partners and extended operations. All partners share ground water, surface water and waste water, steam and electricity, and exchange various products and by-products in a circular approach to production. The figure below depicts a simplified overview of the connections between some of the main partners at Kalundborg. The set-up connects partners from otherwise independent supply chains and generates annual savings of 4 million m^3 ground water, 62,000 tonnes of by-products and waste material and 586,000 tonnes of CO_2.

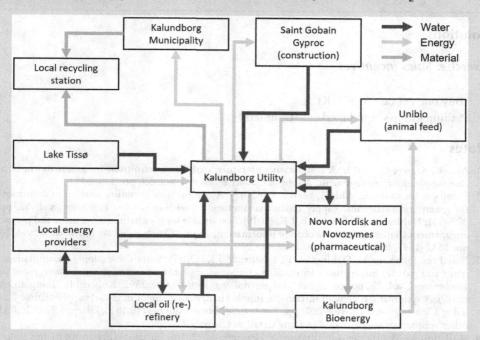

Source: Chertow, Chertow, M.R. (2000). Industrial symbiosis: Literature and taxonomy. *Annual Review of Energy and the Environment*, vol. 25, pp. 313–337.
http://www.symbiosis.dk/en/

Example – L'Oréal

The cosmetics producer L'Oréal has announced a breakthrough in one of their R&D projects aimed at replacing traditional single-use plastic containers. The company announced that they are now able to produce plastic cosmetic bottles using captured carbon with the aim to "make single-use carbon a thing of the past." The project is based on collaboration between three partners: LanzaTech, Total and L'Oréal. LanzaTech captures industrial carbon emissions and converts them into ethanol using a unique biological process. Total then converts this ethanol into ethylene before polymerising it into polyethylene, which has the same technical characteristics as its fossil counterpart. L'Oréal uses this polyethylene to produce packaging with the same quality and properties as conventional polyethylene.

This technological (process) breakthrough paves the way for new opportunities for the capture and reuse of industrial carbon emissions. The partners intend to continue working together on scaling the production of these sustainable plastics and look forward to working with all those who want to join them in committing to the use of new sustainable plastics.

Source: https://www.cips.org/supply-management/news/2020/november/how-loreal-made-the-worlds-first-packaging-using-recycled-carbon-emissions/; https://www.loreal.com/en/news/group/lanzatech-total-and-loreal/

Solutions

Exercise: Sales incentives

- Buy one get one free (UK)
- Salling group's "guldmærker" (Denmark)

Notes

1 Ahi, P., Searcy, C. (2013). A comparative literature analysis of definitions for green and sustainable supply chain management. *Journal of Cleaner Production*, vol. 52, pp. 329–341.
2 Based on, for example, Ahi, P., Searcy, C. (2013). A comparative literature analysis of definitions for green and sustainable supply chain management. *Journal of Cleaner Production*, vol. 52, pp. 329–341; Dahlmann, F., Roehrich, J.K. (2019). Sustainable supply chain management and partner engagement to manage climate change information. *Business Strategy and the Environment*, vol. 28, no. 1632–1647. https://doi.org/10.1002/bse.2392
3 Based on, for example, Dahlmann, F., Roehrich, J.K. (2019). Sustainable supply chain management and partner engagement to manage climate change information. *Business Strategy and the Environment*, vol. 28, pp. 1632–1647. https://doi.org/10.1002/bse.2392; Koberg, E., Longoni, A. (2019). A systematic review of sustainable supply chain management in global supply chains. *Journal of Cleaner Production*, vol. 207, pp. 1084–1098. https://doi.org/10.1016/j.jclepro.2018.10.033; other approaches are discussed in more detail in Chapter 7.
4 Wilhelm, M.M., Blome, C., Bhakoo, V., Paulraj, A. (2016). Sustainability in multi-tier supply chains: Understanding the double agency role of the first-tier supplier. *Journal of Operations Management*, vol. 41, pp. 42–60. https://doi.org/10.1016/j.jom.2015.11.001
5 Kumar, G., Subramanian, N., Maria Arputham, R. (2018). Missing link between sustainability collaborative strategy and supply chain performance: Role of dynamic capability. *International Journal of Production Economics*, vol. 203, pp. 96–109. https://doi.org/10.1016/j.ijpe.2018.05.031
6 Based on Daghar, A., Alinaghian, L., Turner, N. (2021). The role of collaborative interorganizational relationships in supply chain risks: A systematic review using a social capital perspective, *Supply Chain Management*, vol. 26, pp. 279–296. https://doi.org/10.1108/SCM-04-2020-0177
7 Based on Cao, Zhang. (2010). Supply chain collaboration: Impact on collaborative advantage and firm performance. *Journal of Operations Management*, vol. 29, no. 3, pp. 163–180.
8 Based on Daghar, A., Alinaghian, L., Turner, N. (2021). The role of collaborative interorganizational relationships in supply chain risks: A systematic review using a social capital perspective. *Supply Chain Management*, vol. 26, pp. 279–296; Krause, D.R., Handfield, R.B., Tyler, B.B. (2006). The relationships between supplier development, commitment, social capital accumulation and performance improvement. *Journal of Operations Management*. vol. 25, no. 2, pp. 528–545.

7
SUSTAINABLE SOURCING AND PROCUREMENT

Sourcing defines all activities related to obtaining and managing the supply an organisation needs for its daily operations. Through the selected approach to sourcing, a company can directly affect sustainability performance in part of the supply chain. This outcome is usually achieved through the purchasing or procurement functions, which are responsible for providing the input and therefore constitute the vital link between operations and suppliers. Integrating sustainability, especially environmental sustainability performance, into procurement can be relatively straightforward through the following strategies:

- *Reduce the quantity of purchased products and materials:* Traditional approaches to purchasing based on ordering the same number of items without considering actual demand often result in overstocking and waste. Instead, buying firms can implement need-based purchasing and reduce the quantity of purchased items.
- *Reconsider conventional purchases and identify alternative solutions:* With new solutions and sustainable products becoming available, old solutions can often be replaced by sustainable alternatives. The buying firm needs to question and challenge "old" solutions to a specific need. This assessment process can be achieved by establishing systematic monitoring activity of the supply market to identify alternative products or even different ways in which a given need can be fulfilled.
- *Specify green and social products:* The more accurately a buying firm can specify its actual needs, the better a procurement manager can identify solutions that can fulfil these needs without exceeding them with overengineered products or materials.
- *Redesign the product:* Through redesigning a product with sustainable performance criteria in mind (see Part I Introduction and Chapter 2), procurement requirements can be revised with more sustainable performance in mind.

While attempts to include sustainability in procurement often focus on the environmental dimension through efforts such as "greening the supply process" and "product based green supply,"[1] efforts at including social sustainability are also evident. One example is presented in the Box "Tool: UN decent work toolkit for sustainable procurement."

DOI: 10.4324/9781003345077-12

Tool: UN decent work toolkit for sustainable procurement

The United Nations (UN) offers a toolkit for sustainable procurement, which consists of three tools to aid in embedding decent work in the supply chain. Tool 1 focuses on decent work for all and enables supply and procurement managers to explore how their procurement practices and decisions impact working conditions in their global supply chains. Tool 2 focuses on the communication of decent work to suppliers and Tool 3 on embedding decent work in corporate processes. The toolkit aims at enabling companies to incorporate decent work into their global supply chains and to create a positive company and brand image through business responsibility.

Source: https://sustainableprocurement.unglobalcompact.org/

Procurement process

To incorporate sustainability principles into procurement, the procurement process must be understood in terms of the main activities and goals. The procurement process consists of multiple steps and includes[2] shaping the purchasing strategy, vendor pre-selection, vendor selection and relationship and contract management. Figure 7.1 depicts the process. The reverse arrows indicate (a) a processual characteristic, as the process is reinitiated when a contractual term is finished, and (b) a learning characteristic, as continuous improvement efforts aim to learn from experience and improve process steps.

Sourcing strategy

Depending on the needs of the company and pre-defined specification, different sourcing and supply strategies may be applied or combined. Two fundamental sourcing strategies typically deployed in companies are the following:

- Single sourcing defines the approach whereby one supplier supplies a purchased item. Depending on the industry context, this supplier might be the only one available (sole sourcing) or was chosen despite other suppliers being available.
- Multi-sourcing defines the approach whereby more than one independent supplier supplies a good or a service. This strategy is often used in competitive markets with low switching costs and a primary focus on price and dependability.

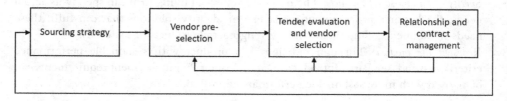

FIGURE 7.1 Procurement process. Based on, for example, Park, J., Shin, K., Chang, T.W., Park, J. (2010). An integrative framework for supplier relationship management. *Industrial Management & Data Systems*, vol. 110, pp. 495–515. https://doi.org/10.1108/02635571011038990; Belvedere, V., Grando, A. (2017). *Sustainable Operations and Supply Chain Management*. Wiley, Chapter 4.

Both approaches exhibit advantages and disadvantages that may make them particularly useful and applicable to specific sourcing decisions and environmental conditions. Table 7.1 lists some of these advantages and disadvantages.

A third sourcing strategy, which comprises a combination of the above-described two strategies, is parallel sourcing. Through parallel sourcing, a focal organisation forms a single source relationship for a component or service for a specific model and sources the same component or service from a different supplier for a different model or service package. This strategy means that the focal organisation can switch to an alternative supplier, who supplies the same component for different models.

Vendor pre-selection

To shortlist vendors, standard accreditation and certifications can form a useful basis to ensure that certain operating and supply thresholds are met. The following standards offer accreditation that is useful for this purpose:

*   *ISO 14000*: voluntary series of international standards on environmental management. The standard defines requirements of environmental management systems (EMS) to enhance environmental performance, demonstrate conformance through a third-party certification and achieve compliance with environmental laws and regulations by means of a voluntary accreditation.

TABLE 7.1 Advantages and disadvantages of single and multiple sourcing[a]

	Advantages	Disadvantages
Single sourcing	The supplier can concentrate on production processes and may hence deliver better quality	The purchaser is more vulnerable to disruption should a failure occur
	This approach may lead to stronger, more durable relationships	Volume fluctuations may affect individual suppliers to a greater extent
	This approach creates greater dependency and encourages more commitment and effort	The supplier might exert upward pressure on prices if no alternative supplier is available
	Single sourcing may lead to better and more open communication	This approach is quite different from sole sourcing, which occurs when there is only one supplier available
	It may be easier to cooperate with a single supplier and share ideas on new product development	
	Single sourcing offers the possibility of economies of scale or, more importantly, the opportunity for the supplier to choose the production quantity, which may differ from the order quantity	
	Partners in a single sourcing arrangement may develop higher confidentiality and trust	
Multi-sourcing	The purchaser can drive the price down by competitive tendering	It is difficult to encourage commitment to supply
	The purchaser can switch sources in case of supply shortage or failure	It is less easy to develop effective quality assurance
	The purchaser has access to a wider source of knowledge and expertise	Suppliers and customers need more effort to communicate effectively
		Suppliers are less likely to invest in new processes
		It is more difficult to obtain economies of scale

Based on Gardiner, D., Reefke, H. (2020). *Operations Management for Business Excellence: Building Sustainable Supply Chains.* Routledge, pp. 330–332.

- *EMAS (Eco-Management and Audit Scheme)*: management tool for evaluating, reporting and improving environmental performance. This tool enables acquisition of information about the environmental performance of private and public organisations.
- *ISO 50001*: voluntary accreditation for improving energy efficiency. The standards aims to enable organisations to make better use of their energy-consuming assets by promoting energy-efficient technology and behaviours.
- *Social Accountability 8000*: accredits ethical behaviour of companies in the following areas: child labour, forced and compulsory labour, health and safety, freedom of association and right to collective bargaining, discrimination, disciplinary practices, working hours and remuneration. This standard establishes appropriate procedures to evaluate and select suppliers/sub-contractors (and, whenever possible, sub-suppliers) based on their ability to meet these requirements, which are also compliant with the International Labour Standards (ILO).
- *Occupational Health and Safety Assessment Series (OHSAS) 18001*: standard concerning the occupational health and safety management system. This standard aims to help organisations to control occupational health and safety risks, enhancing their performance in these areas.

An example of how vendor pre-selection can be useful is described in the Box "Example – Porsche and renewable energy."

Tender evaluation and vendor selection

Sustainability criteria can be integrated into tender evaluations to ensure that sustainable performance outcomes are considered in sourcing decisions. These sustainability criteria extend traditional tender evaluation criteria, which typically include the following[3]:

- Cost: low initial price, compliance with cost analysis system, cost reduction activities and compliance with sectoral price behaviour.

Example – Porsche and renewable energy

Porsche announced that as of July 2021, they require their 1,300 series suppliers to use exclusively renewable energy in the manufacture of Porsche components. This effort aims to reduce the CO_2 emissions in the sports car manufacturer's supply chain. In their announcement, Porsche stated: "It applies to any contracts awarded for providing production material for new vehicle projects. Suppliers who are unwilling to switch to certified green energy will no longer be considered for contracts with Porsche in the long term." This effort marks one step toward the company's goal to be CO_2-neutral across their entire value chain by 2030. For this purpose, Porsche is investing more than a billion euros in decarbonisation measures over the next 10 years. The sports car manufacturer's supply chain is currently responsible for around 20% of Porsche's total greenhouse gas emissions. This figure will increase to 40% by 2030 due to the increasing electrification of vehicles.

Source: https://newsroom.porsche.com/en/2021/sustainability/porsche-co2-neutral-balance-2030-suppliers-switch-green-energy-24971.html

- Quality: conformance quality, consistent delivery, quality philosophy and prompt response.
- Time: delivery speed, product development time and partnership formation time.
- Flexibility: product volume changes, short set-up time, conflict resolution and service capability.
- Innovativeness: new launch of products and new use of technologies.
- Culture: feeling of trust, management attitude and degree of future outlook, strategic fit, top management compatibility, compatibility among levels and functions and suppliers' organisational structure and personnel.
- Technology: technological compatibility, assessment of future manufacturing capabilities, suppliers' speed in development, suppliers' design capability, technical capability and current manufacturing facilities/capabilities.
- Relationship: long-term relationship, relationship closeness, communication openness and reputation for integrity.

Sustainability-related criteria can be added to such tender evaluations. Criteria for evaluating different aspects of environmental sustainability include the following:

- *Environmental practices*: pollution controls (remediation, end-of-pipe controls), pollution prevention (product adaptation, process adaptation), environmental management system (establishment of environmental commitment and policy), identification of environmental aspects, planning of environmental objectives and assignment of environmental responsibility (checking and evaluation of environmental activities).
- *Environmental performance*: resource consumption (consumption of energy, consumption of raw material, consumption of water) and pollution production (production of polluting agents, production of toxic products, production of waste).

As described in Chapter 6 on "Collaborative supply chains," environmental criteria lend themselves to formal assessment, as they can often be evaluated on the sourced component. Such criteria can therefore be included in tender evaluation and vendor selection more easily than social sustainability criteria. While social sustainability criteria can be and often are also included in supplier selection, evaluating compliance can be difficult and is often done in close (long-term) collaboration with a supplier.

Relationship and contract management

Evaluating supplier performance is traditionally often based on arms-length assessments of actual performance against target performance to identify shortcomings. In collaborative supply chains, however, the aim of relationship management is to enable suppliers to "own sustainability." Collaborative activities are based on enabling suppliers to become proactive, inspect their own operations and disclose sustainability issues or remediate them voluntarily. There are various approaches for achieving this dynamic.

One approach is the use of supplier visits and audits, which verify the reliability of the information provided by the supplier and can be especially useful for monitoring performance criteria that cannot be (easily) directly measured by the buyer. Auditing can be conducted by the buyer or by third parties. Audit outcomes can trigger improvement programmes with suppliers through which relevant opportunities are identified. However, in a survey of 900 factories across 50 countries, audits were identified as a source of an adversarial relationship between supplier and buyer. Audits encourage suppliers to focus on minimum-effort compliance rather than a collaborative relationship to create win-win situations and ongoing improvements.[4] This effect limits the usefulness of supplier visits and audits for creating long-term collaborative relationships for sustainable performance.

A second approach is the use of supplier workshops and conferences aimed at creating a community among suppliers and sub-contractors working toward achieving sustainability performance. These workshops and conferences aim to stimulate the sharing and dissemination of practices among suppliers and with the buyer firm. Suppliers can, for example, describe their various sustainability initiatives and projects and the results they have achieved. Workshop discussions can engage supply chain partners about lessons learned from these initiatives and the viability of developed solutions in other contexts.

A third approach is supplier social and environmental training, whereby the buyer firm supports their suppliers' sustainability paths through training programmes and workshops. This role is typically assumed by large companies, which support smaller suppliers and sub-contractors. It requires significant investment in financial and human resources. The aim is to raise awareness and enable implementation of best practices with suppliers.

The different approaches can be combined to achieve performance improvements. The Box "Example – Nike's sustainable manufacturing and sourcing index (SMSI)" describes how Nike combines different approaches in supplier relationship management.

Example – Nike's sustainable manufacturing and sourcing index (SMSI)

In addition to audits, Nike has implemented various incentives for suppliers to improve their sustainability performance aligned with the sport apparel manufacturer's own values. Among these efforts, Nike created a sustainable manufacturing and sourcing index (SMSI) index, whereby they rate suppliers based on their performance across the equally weighed factors of quality, on-time delivery, costs and sustainability. This ranking applies only to the tier 1 factories.

Nike rates their suppliers as gold, silver, bronze, yellow and red. If a supplier's performance falls below Nike's minimum compliance standards, they receive a yellow or red rating. A bronze rating indicates baseline compliance, meaning that the supplier shares the company's commitment to the welfare of workers and is using resources responsibly and efficiently. The supplier requires additional work across environment, labour and health and safety. Silver signals that a facility is enhancing its sustainability capabilities as a business driver within the industry. Gold indicates what Nike would consider to be a world-class facility in sustainability in any industry.

Nike also collaborates with external partners, such as the Social Labor Convergence Program (SLCP) and the Fair Labor Association and Better Work, and participates in the Sustainable Apparel Coalition's Facility Environmental Module (FEM). Partnerships like the Leadership Group for Responsible Recruitment and the Responsible Business Alliance provide the tools and collective leverage to drive change in different sustainability performance areas with a predominant focus on social values, such as the reduction of excessive overtime, wages and benefits.

Source: https://purpose-cms-preprod01.s3.amazonaws.com/wp-content/
uploads/2020/02/11230637/FY19-Nike-Inc.-Impact-Report.pdf

Contracts play an important role in most inter-organisational relationships, as they define and frame the engagement between buyer and supplier. Contracts typically function as complements to relational engagements. In the context of achieving sustainable performance with suppliers, contracts are expected to play an even more important role in the future, as described in the Box "Note: Contract management."

Note: Contract management

Large, globally operating firms invest in their legal departments and in contractual capabilities in order to maximise their credentials in sustainability performance and to ensure that they meet their environmental and social sustainability pledges. In-house lawyers play an important role in achieving these targets, as they often manage contract renegotiations with suppliers and manage regulatory compliance. As supply chains play an increasingly crucial role in achieving sustainability pledges, legal departments need closer involvement with procurement and sourcing practices, including reporting and disclosure. Contractual provisions now increasingly include clauses on environmental, social and governance (ESG) commitments or a link to the supplier's code of conduct with requirements for sharing information to create transparency. The companies that get this wrong risk failure in the public eye.

Source: *The Financial Times*. https://amp.ft.com/content/a35776c3-d263-4b4e-ae10-3985c386b058; June 2021

Sourcing portfolio analysis

Buying firms often deal with a large number of suppliers. For example, Siemens has more than 400 tier 1 suppliers, who in turn have more than 3,000 tier 2 suppliers (for Siemens). Similarly, Ford Motor company has 1,500 tier 1 suppliers and tens of thousands of deeper tier suppliers. Flex procures 700,000 parts from 14,000 tier 1 suppliers. Driving sustainability performance across these suppliers requires a nuanced approach, as seen in the Box "Example – Sustainability in the value chain of renewable energy at Vestas."

Example – Sustainability in the value chain of renewable energy at Vestas

In their sustainability strategy, Vestas aims to reduce carbon emissions across their supplier network by 45% per MWh of wind energy delivered to the market. This ambitious aim comes in a context of increasing demand for wind turbines and equipment, as many countries seek to increase their share of renewable energy production. For Vestas, the result is a need to scale up their operations and increase procurement activities across their value chain. To reach their aim, Vestas has initiated a two-step process in their supply chain management. First, they target supply chain transparency and incentivise carbon emission reduction with a sub-set of 27 strategic suppliers that represent 30% of the company's material spend. These strategic suppliers were asked to implement a set of activities ranging from powering their own operations through using 100% renewable energy to reporting on CO_2 emissions and production waste for the products purchased by Vestas. This set of strategic suppliers also committed to ambitious emission targets for their own operations. Second, Vestas works with these strategic suppliers to reduce their Scope 3 emissions. Vestas will support them in this journey by sharing insights from their own journey on this path. This support includes webinars for the suppliers, guidance in calculating carbon footprints and focusing their annual supplier forum on the topic of sustainability. Vestas hopes that these activities combined will enable them to take the next steps in achieving their ambitious targets together with their suppliers.

Source: Vestas blogpost "Accelerating sustainability performance across the renewable value chain". https://www.vestas.com/en/media/blog/sustainability/acclerating-sustainability-performance-across-the-renewable-value-chain, March 2021.

To manage large supplier bases, supplier segmentation offers the ability to effectively identify the requirements of key groups of suppliers and develop approaches to managing relationships with them. Supplier segments can be defined based on different criteria. One criterion to consider is the "importance" of the supplier, which can be assessed in various ways. A typical approach to analysing a supplier portfolio considers both the value potential of the supplied components, materials or services on the one hand and the potential impact that a disruption in supply would cause on the other. These two dimensions produce a 2x2 matrix when analysing each dimension as high or low, as depicted in Table 7.2.[5] The four resulting supplier segments are bottleneck, critical, routine and leverage, with different effects on the buying firm's ability to drive sustainability performance. See Box "Exercise: Driving sustainability with supplier segments."

Exercise: Driving sustainability with supplier segments

Have a look at the characteristics of the different supplier segments in Table 7.2. How can a buying firm drive sustainability performance across the supply chain with suppliers in the four segments?

TABLE 7.2 Supplier portfolio analysis

		Value potential	
		Low	High
Potential impact	High	**Bottleneck:** Complex specifications requiring a complex manufacturing or service process. Few alternative products/sources of supply. Significant impact on operations/maintenance. New technology or untested processes	**Critical:** Critical to profitability and operations. Few qualified sources of supply. Large expenditures. Design and quality critical. Complex and/or rigid specification

Low	Routine:	Leverage:
	Many alternative products and services	Large expenditures, commodity items
	Many sources of supply	
	Low value, small individual transactions	Large marketplace capacity, ample inventories
	Everyday use, unspecified items	
	Anyone could buy it	Many alternative products and services
		Many qualified sources of supply
		Market/price sensitive

A "bottleneck" supplier fulfils unique or complex requirements that can only be met by few suppliers. Here, the primary goal of the sourcing strategy is to ensure supply continuity by not running out of the procured item or service. This goal might result in carrying additional inventory to reduce supply risk. The buying firm is dependent on the supplier and hence has a limited ability to drive sustainability initiatives.

A critical supplier fulfils complex or unique requirements which can be fulfilled by few other suppliers. The main difference from the "bottleneck" segment is the substantial level of expenditure for the sourcing firm. This level of expenditure means that they spend considerable time negotiating favourable deals and building long-term partnerships with suppliers. Buying firms also often prepare contingency plans for managing supply disruptions. Here, sustainability can be increased through supplier cooperation.

Routine suppliers are readily available and represent a small portion of a firm's purchasing expenditures. Examples are suppliers of office supplies and cleaning services. The sourcing strategy often aims at simplifying the acquisition process and lowering costs, for example, through automation or reducing the number of suppliers. In this segment, vendor accreditation and other criteria in vendor pre-selection represent useful tools to drive sustainability performance.

A leverage supplier supplies standardised products or services that are readily available in the market but represent a significant portion of spend. Here, the buying firm's sourcing strategy focuses on leveraging the firm's spending levels to achieve the most favourable terms possible. The buying firm may define preferred suppliers, allowing them to apply elimination criteria in vendor pre-selection. Sustainability performance can be driven through collaboration and a procurement process based on sustainability performance criteria.

Vertical integration

When supplier development or supplier management is not possible or practical, an alternative approach to achieving sustainable performance is vertical integration. Vertical integration defines the process whereby a firm extends its existing operational processes to include upstream or downstream process steps. Figure 7.2 illustrates the logic of vertical integration, which can include forward or backward integration. In backward integration, a firm develops the ability to produce goods or services it previously purchased from vendors or suppliers. In other words, a firm decides to make what it previously bought. An example is described in the Box "Example – Vertical integration at Dr Bronner's." In forward integration, a firm moves downstream and develops the abilities to deliver

process steps that were previously handled by downstream supply partners. One example here is servitization (Chapter 5), whereby a manufacturing firm moves downstream and provides operational support services for its manufactured products or equipment.

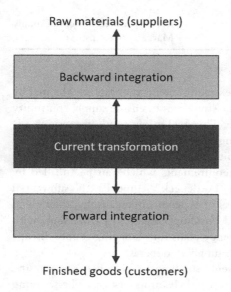

FIGURE 7.2   Vertical integration, including backward and forward integration. Based on Heizer, J., Render, B., Munson, C. (2020). *Operations Management: Sustainability and Supply Chain Management.* Pearson, Global edition, p. 480.

Example – Vertical integration at Dr. Bronner's

Through its Fair for Life programme, Dr. Bronner's started to align its supply chain with its beliefs by sourcing only certified Fairtrade ingredients. However, the soap maker ran into problems with coconut and palm oils, as they could not verify the labour and environmental practices behind production, resulting in a traceability issue in their supply chain. The supply chain consists of growers, producers and brokers, and the brokers were not able to provide the information that Dr. Bronner's needed for their sustainability programme.

Dr. Bronner's response was vertical integration to bypass brokers and gain direct access to the supply of their materials. They built a mill in Ghana and acquired a coconut oil processing facility in Sri Lanka. They then sourced the oil they needed only from local smallholder farmers whose practices the company approved. While this approach enabled the transparency Dr. Bronner's craved, it also increased business risks and costs. This approach exposed the company to supply shortages from its suppliers during bad years. To overcome this issue, Dr. Bronner's needed to make different investments. In the beginning, the company needed to pay the start-up costs to bring mills up to their standards. In the first year, they even had to prepay for crops that were not even planted yet. This obligation in turn required them to improve their prediction and forecasting abilities. The company needed to map their ingredient usage over a four-year horizon. Vertical integration has enabled Dr. Bronner's to take charge of its supply chain and improve sustainability performance.

Source: Sheffi, Y., Blanco, E. (2018). *Balancing Green: When to Embrace Sustainability in a Business (and When Not To)*. MIT Press, Chapter 11.

Notes

1 Seuring, S., Müller, M. (2008). From a literature review to a conceptual framework for sustainable supply chain management. *Journal of Cleaner Production*, vol. 16, pp. 1699–1710. https://doi.org/10.1016/j.jclepro.2008.04.020
2 Based on, for example, Jongkyung, P., Shin, K., Chang, T.W., Park, J. (2010). An integrative framework for supplier relationship management. *Industrial Management & Data Systems*, vol. 110, pp. 495–515.
3 Dou, Y., Sarkis, J. (2010). A joint location and outsourcing sustainability analysis for a strategic offshoring decision. *International Journal of Production Research*, vol. 48, no. 2, pp. 567–592.
4 Locke, R. M. (2013). *The Promise and Limits of Private Power*, Cambridge University Press, Cambridge.
5 Based on Bozarth, C.C., Handfield, R.B. (2019). *Introduction to Operations and Supply Chain Management*. Pearson, Global Edition, p. 225.

8

SUSTAINABLE TRANSPORT AND LOGISTICS

Transport and logistics hold a strong potential for sustainability performance. The 2014 IPCC report indicates that globally, 14% of all direct and 0.3% of all indirect greenhouse gas (GHG) emissions are generated by transport. The World Resource Institute states that the transport sector accounted for 7.9 billion tonnes of CO_2 emissions in 2016 (accounting for 21% of the global total CO_2 emissions were 36.7 billion tonnes in the same year). In other databases, the relative contribution can account for up to 24% of global total emissions. This means that transport and logistics management can hold a large potential for lowering environmental impacts in supply chains.

Logistics management

Logistics management constitutes a part of supply chain management, which is concerned with planning, implementing and controlling the efficiency and effective flow and storage of goods, services and related information.[1] As such, logistics management includes activities of inbound and outbound transportation management, fleet management, warehousing, materials handling, order fulfilment, logistics network design, inventory management, supply and demand planning and management of third-party logistics (3PL) providers.

The importance of logistics management within current global supply chains cannot be over-emphasised as described in the Box "Note: The supply chain crisis, as told by a stuck box of fertiliser." The quantity of transported freight has increased over recent decades. For example, the total volumes of freight transported in the European Union (EU) between 1995 and 2011 increased by 25%. Logistics management accounts for a substantial percentage of the gross domestic product (GDP) of many countries. Figure 8.1 shows the numbers for some exemplar countries.

DOI: 10.4324/9781003345077-13

Note: The supply chain crisis, as told by a stuck box of fertiliser

At Shanghai port, a box of fertiliser waits for its shipment to the United States of America together with all the other boxes of products to be shipped. It has been sitting there for three months as typhoons and COVID outbreaks caused delays in the world's busiest port. Usually, this trip would take the box of fertiliser only weeks to reach its destination 15,000 km away. But travel times have stretched, as global congestion has gripped global trade and slowed supply chains. Another Chinese port even had to be closed because of a COVID outbreak. It is a similar situation in ports across the globe. And the effects will be visible only months or years from now. The box of fertiliser should have been with a US farmer in April, just when it is needed to start the planting season. Now, this farmer has to make do without it.

The delays started even before the box of fertiliser arrived at the Shanghai port. Waiting at the manufacturing side thousands of kilometres inland from Shanghai, the box already experienced delays as no empty containers were available. These containers were held up because of understaffing, a lack of trucking equipment and many other reasons. Once the box of fertiliser leaves the port of Shanghai, it will face a similar situation at its arrival port and further delays being transported to its final destination.

Source: https://www.supplychainbrain.com/articles/33677-one-stuck-box-of-fertilizer-shows-the-global-supply-chain-crisis, August 2021.

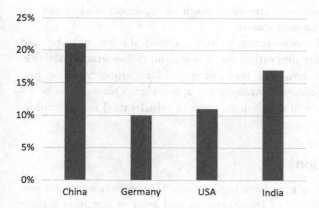

FIGURE 8.1 Logistics costs as a percentage of the GDP of selected countries in 2011. Based on Bozarth, C.C., Handfield, R.B. (2019). *Introduction to Operations and Supply Chain Management*. Pearson, Global edition, p. 243.

These numbers of the logistics costs have actually reduced as efficiency efforts have successfully been implemented. For example, the US logistics costs attributed for 17.9% of GDP in the 1980s and 8.5% in 2013. Efficiencies have been created through the following approaches:

- *Storage, warehousing and materials handling*: optimisation for number of warehouses, their size and location and the type of equipment to use.

- *Inventory*: how much should be stocked, where should inventory be held (e.g., in a central warehouse rather than in local distribution centres) and which items.
- *Transport*: choice of transport mode, the type of delivery operations, load planning and route scheduling.
- *Packaging*: choice of the primary and secondary packaging.
- *Information and control*: effective control systems, enable feedback and feed-forward control process.

Designing physical distribution is an important task and involves strategic (long-term choices), structural, functional and operational choices. Strategic choices present the context for many functional and operational choices discussed later in this chapter. Strategic choices determine speed and dependability of the delivery, availability and completeness of the order. This can also concern required flexibility of order delivery as different options need to be considered. Traditionally, many of these considerations are based on strategic decisions made within the focal organisation. As indicated in the Box "Note: The supply chain crisis, as told by a stuck box of fertiliser" external drivers may pose significant constraints on the ability to achieve some of the strategic choices.

These strategic choices affect structural choices of the physical distribution in terms of distribution channels and organisation of logistics networks. Here, network decisions regarding the number and location of warehouses and depots determine sustainability performance, especially in terms of environmental footprint. These structural choices feed directly into the functional choices regarding management of warehouses, transportation and physical flow of goods. This is also where the mode of transports is defined, which has strong implications for the GHG emissions created through an organisation's logistics system as described in more detail in the next section.

Finally, the operational choices focus on issues, including technical solutions to be used, information technology (IT) systems supporting the storage and transportation activities (such as Warehouse Management Systems and Transportation Management Systems), process management approaches and personnel management approaches. Questions to be addressed here are degree of automation in warehouses, types of vehicles used and technology supporting them.

Modal choices of transportation

Modal choices of transport matter as they have implications for the environmental performance of logistics management, cost of transportation and level of customer service. Despite the increasing total volumes of freight and changes in available technology and infrastructure, the mix of transportation modes has remained largely unchanged for a long time. For example, within the EU 27 states,[2] road transport accounted for 51% as the highest frequented mode of transport in 2018. Intra-EU sea freight scored a second place with 29.2%, which constituted a decrease in comparison to 37.5% in 1995. Air freight was the lowest with only 0.1% of all volumes of freight transport while rail accounted for 12.6%.

In comparison, the GHG emissions from transport paint a radically different picture. Referring to global GHG emissions in the transportation sector 2018, road (freight) transport accounted for 29.4% of the total transport-related emissions, while shipping represented 10.6%. Air (freight) transport comes in third with 2.2%[3] and rail at 1% (the remaining percentages refer to passenger transportation).[4] This shows that the mode of transportation affects environmental sustainability performance. It also affects the other sustainability performance dimensions – economic and social – and is hence of great importance for logistics management.

Choosing the "right" mode of transport is dependent on various constraining factors, both endogenous and exogenous. Endogenous factors are associated with the design choices concerning the physical distribution process. This includes the strategic, structural, functional and operational choices described above. Exogenous factors concern externally determined factors, such as fuel costs, technological innovation (especially in relation to vehicle performance), economic and tax policies, trends of the global economy, the characteristics of the infrastructures of a country and the macro-trends of the development of national economies. Table 8.1 shows a brief overview of the capabilities of the different modes of transport typically used. A particular focus is often the GHG emissions of the different modes of transport. This is described in more detail in the Box "Note: Measuring GHG emissions of modes of transport."

TABLE 8.1 Comparison between different modes of transport[a]

Mode	Strengths	Limitations	Primary global role
Road	Accessibility Fast and versatile Customer service	Limited capacity High cost	Origin-port and port-destination Intermodal container movement Transborder flow of goods between adjacent countries
Air	Fast Freight protection Flexibility High traceability of the shipment	Door-to-door accessibility High cost Low capacity High levels of GHG emissions	Fast movements of high value goods and urgent shipments
Sea	High capacity Low cost Carrier availability	Slow Door-to-door accessibility Low traceability of the shipment	Highly efficient Long distance transfer of containerised finished goods, bulk materials and equipment
Rail	High capacity Low cost	Accessibility Inconsistent service Damage rates	Move large shipments of bulk materials between countries Longer distance port destination, intermodal container movement

a Based on Gibson, B.J., Hanna, Joe, B., Defee, C.C., Chen, H. (2014). *The Definitive Guide to Integrated Supply Chain Management*. Council of Supply Chain Management Professionals, p. 162; Gardiner, D., Reefke, H. (2020). *Operations Management for Business Excellence: Building Sustainable Supply Chain*, 4th ed. Routledge.

Note: Measuring GHG emissions of modes of transport

A simulation study conducted by ecotransit.org aimed to investigate the CO_2 emissions of 100 tonnes of freight along a route on the Mediterranean coast. This route can be alternatively covered by the four modes of transport: air, road, rail and sea and resulted in the outcomes reported in the table below. These outcomes show that while the distances are comparable (about 700 km), the CO_2 emissions vary substantially. While air transport is the most polluting, road transport is about five times as polluting as rail transport. This can form the basis for rethinking the used modes of transportation many organisations as rail is often considered to play a more important role in fleet management in the future.

	Air	Road	Rail	Sea
CO_{2e} (t)	125	5.2	1.0	0.5
Distance (km)	706	701	709	691

Source: Belvedere, V., Grando, A. (2017). *Sustainable Operations and Supply Chain Management*, Chapter 6; https://www.ecotransit.org/en/

In practice, different modes of transport are combined resulting in different combinations of road, air, sea and rail transport in global supply chains. The Box "Tool: LCA of shopping bags – Transportation in the global supply chains" continues the previously introduced example of the life-cycle assessment (LCA) of different options of shopping carrier bags and focuses on the impact of transportation.

Tool: LCA of shopping bags – Transportation in the global supply chains

The UK Environment Agency carried out an LCA of commonly used shopping bags. They compared the following five bags: a lightweight carrier made from high-density polyethylene (HDPE), a "bag for life" made from low-density polyethylene (LDPE), a paper bag, a heavier plastic bag with stiffening inserts made from non-woven polypropylene (PP) and a cotton bag. As part of their study, the analysts estimated the CO_2-equivalent emissions from the production of these four types of bags. In addition to the material flows and energy flows analysed in earlier chapters, the study also traced emissions from transporting the bags across their global supply chains.

The LCA of transport includes the following parts of the supply chain:

* Transportation of the raw materials from the place of extraction or cultivation to the production facility.
* Transportation of carrier bags to carrier bag importer, including transport of secondary packaging materials from their places of extraction or cultivation.
* Transport of carrier bags from carrier bag importer to the supermarket.
* Transport related to disposal of carrier bags through municipal waste collection.

Excluded from the LCA were the consumer transport between the supermarket and their home. Transport distances were calculated based on typical exporting countries for the different bag options. HDPE and PP bags are typically imported to the United Kingdom from Far East countries, such as China, Indonesia and Malaysia. In contrast, 90% LDPE bags are typically imported from Turkey and Germany with the remaining 10% coming from Far East countries. Table 8.I lists the combination of transport modes for the different carrier bags based on typical production and supply chain constellations.

TABLE 8.I Transport scenarios for the carrier bag options

Bag type	Transport from	Heat (from natural gas)	Transport modes	Distance
HDPE bag	Polymer resin producer in Far East	Bag producer in Far East	Road (lorry) Sea	100 km 500 km
	Titanium oxide and chalk producer in Far East	Bag producer in Far East	Road (lorry) Sea	200 km 500 km
	Bag producer in Far East	Bag importer in United Kingdom	Road (lorry) Sea Rail	100 km 15,000 km 280 km
	Bag importer in United Kingdom	Supermarket	Road (lorry)	200 km
Paper bag	Bag producer in Europe	Bag importer in United Kingdom	Road (lorry)	1,000 km
	Bag importer in United Kingdom	Supermarket	Road (lorry)	200 km
Bag for life (LDPE)	Polymer resin producer in Europe	Bag producer in Turkey	Road (lorry)	300 km
	Bag producer in Turkey	Bag importer in United Kingdom	Sea Rail	5,000 km 280 km
	Polymer resin producer in Far East	Bag producer in Far East	Road (lorry) Sea	100 km 500 km
	Titanium oxide producer in Far East	Bag producer in Far East	Road (lorry) Sea	200 km 500 km
	Bag producer in Far East	Bag importer in United Kingdom	Road (lorry) Sea Rail	100 km 15,000 km 280 km
	Bag importer in United Kingdom	Supermarket	Road (lorry)	200 km
PP bag	Polymer resin producer in Far East	Bag producer in Far East	Road (lorry)	100 km
	Bag producer in Far East	Bag importer in United Kingdom	Road (lorry) Sea Rail	100 km 15,000 km 280 km
	Bag importer in United Kingdom	Supermarket	Road (lorry)	200 km
Cotton bag	Textile producer in China	Bag producer in China	Road (lorry)	100 km
	Bag producer in China	Bag importer in United Kingdom	Road (lorry) Sea Rail	100 km 15,000 km 280 km
	Bag importer in United Kingdom	Supermarket	Road (lorry)	200 km

These inputs were used to calculate the global warming potential of the different carrier bag options. Using data about European transport efficiencies with data sets representative of the year 2005 for road transport and of 2000 for all other transportation modes. Considering the number of bags needed to carry an average monthly shop of a UK citizen and the weight of an individual bag, the LCA resulted in the following estimations of global warming potential from transportation for each type of carrier bag (based on IPCC 2007 characterisation factors):

- HDPE bag: 0.18 kg CO_2 equivalent.
- Paper bag: 0.72 kg CO_2 equivalent.
- LDPE bag: 0.32 kg CO_2 equivalent.
- PP bag: 1.95 kg CO_2 equivalent.
- Cotton bag: 3.3 kg CO_2 equivalent.

These impacts are mainly attributed to emissions from road transport. In case of shipping from the Far East, the impact of that shipping accounted for 60%–70% of the transport impact to the global warming potential of the carrier bag. The study also reports estimates on human toxicity, eutrophication, etc., which are highly affected by the mode of transportation.

Source: Edwards, C., Fry, J.M. (2011). Life cycle assessment of supermarket carrier bags: A review of the bags available in 2006. Bristol, UK. https://assets. publishing.service.gov.uk/government/uploads/system/uploads/attachment_ data/file/291023/scho0711buan-e-e.pdf

Improving sustainability of transport choices

Most processes for improving sustainability performance tend to be focused on the environmental dimension. However, many of these approaches enable targeting of multiple dimensions of the sustainability definition as described in the Box "Note: Alignment between economic and environmental sustainability performance."

Note: Alignment between economic and environmental sustainability performance

A report published by the Corporate Partnerships Program in the Environmental Defence Fund gives companies concise advice on how to manage their global logistics networks by saving costs and reducing GHG emissions. The report collects stories and best practices of different companies, including Nike, Wal-Mart and Ikea and collates them to present a list of actions that companies can take to improve their distribution and logistics networks. The target audience is companies that utilise logistics networks to move products but whose main activities fall outside of the freight business. One of the main cost factors for these companies is the price of fuel – so reducing the use of fuel in their logistics networks has the potential for creating massive savings. This is an example where the driver to reduce costs is well aligned with environmental sustainability performance improvements.

Source: https://www.forbes.com/sites/justingerdes/2012/02/24/how–nike– wal-mart-and-ikea-are-saving-money-and-slashing-carbon-by-shipping– smarter/?sh=30b32baf5687

To improve the environmental sustainability of transport choices, a baseline needs to be identified to which to compare any improvement efforts. This can be done via carbon footprint auditing, which defines the process of quantifying the total amount of carbon dioxide and other GHG (typically expressed in CO_2 equivalents – CO_{2e}), which are emitted directly or indirectly by an entity. The reasons for conducting carbon foot auditing can be various. It can be a necessity to comply with mandatory reporting programs set out by governmental authorities or to give the possibility of participating in GHG markets. It can also be the basis for identifying and implementing actions and initiatives that aim to improve the environmental footprint of the company.

In a second step, transportation waste can be eliminated. Here, the lean approach (see Chapter 4) offers a meaningful basis. The logistics manager needs to set relevant improvement targets and plan appropriate actions as follows:

1   All activities and processes that require transportation need to be identified. This includes external and internal activities and processes.
2   The mode of transport needs to be specified, including the distances to be covered.[5] This enables the logistics manager to gain a picture of the current state.
3   Possible solutions to reducing the environmental impact of transportation need to be identified. This includes, for example, shifts in modes of transport (e.g., from air to sea, from road to rail, etc.). This can also include the implementation to new and less polluting technologies, reducing the need for transportation (through local sourcing) and similar potential solutions. Further options can be identified – see, for example, the Box "Exercise: Reduce environmental impact of transport."
4   The remaining negative effects of transportation can be offset through market measures.

Exercise: Reduce environmental impact of transport

What can companies do to reduce environmental impact of the transport related to their business?

Shift of transport modes

Shifting modes of transportation offers immediate improvements in sustainability performance, such as reduction in CO_2 emissions. Where these benefits are obvious and relatively easily achievable, they have been implemented in industry. The boxes below describe two examples of shift in transportation modes and the related improvements in sustainability performance. Both examples reiterate alignment between improving economic and environmental sustainability dimensions.

Example 1: Shift in transport modes – Natural Resource Defense Council (NRDC)

Natural Resource Defense Council (NRDC, a US non-governmental organisation) revealed that the faster transportation often also results in higher CO_2 emissions and is more expensive. NRDC calculated the emissions created by transporting a t shirt from the Chinese cotton growing region of Xinjiang to consumers in Denver, Colorado. In scenario 1, the transportation modes required transportation by road (truck), air and road, while scenario 2 focused on transportation by rail, sea and rail. Based on 2012 data, they identified the following time requirements:

Scenario 1: Road + air + road: 1 week
Scenario 2: Rail + ship + rail: 4–5 weeks

However, scenario 1 also created 35 times as many CO_2 emissions as scenario 2.

Based on investigations like these, NRDC has launched a larger Clean by Design effort. This effort is aimed at supporting national governments to monitor manufacturing or enforce environmental standards to enable responsible sourcing. For this responsible sourcing initiative (RSI), NRDC partnered with seven multinational apparel retailers and brands. To date, they have achieved a high contribution of textiles industry to emissions.

Source: Sheffi, Y., Blanco, E. (2018). *Balancing Green: When to Embrace Sustainability in a Business (and When Not To)*. MIT Press, Chapter 6; https://www.nrdc.org/resources/green-textile-redux-clean-designs-10-best-practices-offer-even-greater-pollution-reduction

Example 2: Shift in transport modes – Continental clothing and Levi's

Since Continental clothing implemented a "no air freight" policy, they have slashed 90% of GHG emissions for some of its products. Similarly, Levi's implemented a change in transportation modes in their supply chains. Motivated by cost savings, they use less air and truck travel and instead rely more on sea and rail. With this, they have reduced the GHG emissions by 50%–60%.

Source: Sheffi, Y., Blanco, E. (2018). *Balancing Green: When to Embrace Sustainability in a Business (and When Not To)*. MIT Press, Chapter 6.

Efforts within the industry sectors related to each mode of transport also aim to increase sustainability performance. Many of these efforts focus around reducing the environmental impacts of using a specific mode of transport. One example – sea transport – is described in the following section.

Current sustainability developments – the case of maritime

Sea transport forms a vital part of global supply chains. The United National Conference on Trade and Development (UNCTAD) estimates that about 90% of the volume of world trade and about 70% of its value pass sea travel via maritime transport. The many different kinds of ships operating around the globe at this moment stretch from gas transport to container ships and include about 60,000 commercial vessels (like ferries) and about 100,000 smaller vessels for fishing.

Sustainable maritime transport as defined by the UNCTAD aims to create acceptable environmental performance of the maritime supply chain while also respecting traditional economic performance criteria.[6] Social criteria are often implicitly integrated into these criteria. Maritime transport is governed by the International Maritime Organization (IMO), which is a specialised agency of the United Nations and regulated shipping.

The IMO formalised an Initial GHG Strategy in 2018,[7] which focused on the reduction of GHG emissions from ships and sets out a vision for international shipping. Specifically, the IMO aims to reduce annual GHG emissions by at least 50% by 2050 (in comparison to 2008 levels) and reduce the annual CO_2 emissions per transport work by at least 40% by 2030, pursuing efforts towards reaching 70% by 2050. To meet the timelines identified in the initial IMO strategy, the IMO defined a set of measures which can be largely categorised as follows:

- Short-term measures (until 2023): These include a combination of technological and operational measures.
- Medium-term measures (2023–2030): These focus largely on market-based measures, including emissions trading schemes (EMS) and carbon tax or levy on fuel.
- Long-term measures (2030–2050): These focus on developing and implementing alternative fuels.

Technical and operational measures aim to ensure efficiency in maritime transport through increasing the efficiency of engines and propulsion systems, improving ship designs, using cleaner fuels (low sulphur content), using alternative fuels (fuel cells, biofuels, etc.), applying devices to vessels that would trap exhaust emissions (such as scrubbers), implementing energy recuperation devices and applying "cold ironing" in ports, to name some examples. Logistics-based measures focus around, for example, speed reduction, optimised routing and fleet management. National innovation programmes create industry competitiveness through accelerating the development and implementation of new technologies and solutions. One example is the Danish Blue INNOship,[8] which resulted in many new technologies brought to the market.

Market-based measures aim to make the polluter pay for the GHG emissions. Market-based measures encourage vessel operators and investors to adopt measures that reduce CO_2 emissions – rather than prescribing these measures. For example, market-based measures can encourage a ship owner to buy an energy-efficient ship or use low carbon fuel. The financial burden can hence function to bridge the gap between existing (high-carbon) fuels and alternative fuels. The collected finances can be used for various purposes, including investments in technological advancements (direct or in-sector investments) and environmental initiatives (indirect or out-of-sector initiatives).

Outlook

Rolling these measures from sustainable shipping out to other transport modes poses specific challenges, not least based on technological development in these areas. For example, in aviation, we currently do not have the technologies to decarbonise air traffic. New product designs emerge and are being developed. One example is described in the Box "Example: Miners experiment with hydrogen to power giant trucks." Similarly, in other modes of transport, solutions on how to reduce emissions exist and are being scaled.[9]

Example: Miners experiment with hydrogen to power giant trucks

Anglo American is piloting the retrofitting of one of their 220 tonne mining haul trucks with hydrogen power technology. Initially, the truck is hybrid, with a hydrogen fuel cell providing about 50% of the power in combination with a battery pack. In usual set-ups, these trucks can consume 134 litres of diesel per hour and retrofitting hydrogen technology offers substantial benefits, not only economically but also environmentally.

In the retrofitted state, the truck emits only water vapour and the potential savings in on-site emissions are estimated to be 80%. Once scaled, this solution will offer Anglo American the potential of saving the equivalent emissions of half a million diesel cars.

Source: https://www.bbc.co.uk/news/business-59576867.amp, December 2021.

Transport demand is expected to grow further in the coming years and decades. This is partially due to the mega trends described in the introduction. For example, through global population growth, more people will want and need to travel and will need to consume goods. In combination with new technologies, this may increase the environmental impact as a recent study by ETH Zurich reports (see Box "Example: How micromobility affects the climate"). The International Energy Agency described in their Energy Technology Perspectives report their expectation for global transport to double by 2070. This includes, for example, the demand on air travel (passenger and freight) to triple. To offset this increase in demand, technological solutions are expected to play a major role in the future. This includes electrification and hydrogen to decarbonise road and rail transport. Many countries in the EU, the United States of America, China and Japan are expected to phase out conventional vehicles as soon as 2040. Other technologies are still to be developed or scaled for commercial availability. The effects of these technologies are hence impossible to predict.

Example: How micromobility affects the climate

Researchers at ETH Zurich studied the environmental effects of using electric micromobility technologies, such as e-scooters or e-bikes, for person transport. Their study shows that these solutions emit more CO_2 emissions than the alternatives they replace. The reasons can be found in the lifecycle of these technologies and the change in user behaviour; specifically, substitution patterns of these technologies. E-scooters and e-bikes typically substitute cleaner modes of transport, such as walking, public transport or cycling.

Source: https://ethz.ch/en/news-and-events/eth-news/news/2022/01/how-micromobility-affects-climate.html, January 2022.

Solutions

Exercise: Reduce environmental impact of transport

- Advances in vehicles technology → sustainable transport, for example, use of electric and hybrid cars.
- Training for employees to change their driving behaviour, for example, more defensive driving style that also reduces fuel consumption.
- Incentives for their employees to use alternative transport means, for example, rail transport instead of flying.
- Servitization can help here, too (e.g., Michelin case, similar company, e.g., Volvo).
- Local sourcing: reduces vulnerability in the supply chain; but even so, sometimes increased carbon footprint (example in Sheffi).
- Delivery planning and service-level agreements: higher load factor, using bigger vehicles.
  - But constraints: customer's demand variability (Lecture 08).
- Fleet management: volume and delivery flexibility (vehicles used: small vans vs. large trucks).
- Carbon offset: financial support of initiatives beneficial for environment (production of renewable energies, reforestation programs, biodiversity protection, etc.).

Notes

1 Based on CSCMP. (2021). Council of supply chain management professionals—Supply Chain Management Definitions and Glossary [WWW Document]. https://cscmp.org/CSCMP/Educate/SCM_Definitions_and_Glossary_of_Terms.aspx
2 Values based on 2018 numbers published in the EU Statistical Pocketbook 2020.
3 While air transport often gets a lot of attention in discussions around GHG emissions, it has a relatively low contribution to global GHG emissions in the transport sector. However, its contribution to global warming is undenied not only as a result of the CO_2 emissions from burning fuel but also because planes affect the concentration of other gases and pollutants with short-term increases but long-term decreases in ozone, decrease in methane, emissions of water vapour, etc. Some of these impacts result in warming while others create a cooling effect.
4 ourworldindata.com, sourced from the International Energy Agency (IEA).
5 More detailed list of tools can be found in, for example, Wills, B. (2009). *Green intentions: Creating a Green Value Stream to Compete and Win.* CRC Press, New York.
6 Compare this definition to the earlier definitions of eco-effectiveness and eco-efficiency.
7 https://www.imo.org/en/MediaCentre/HotTopics/Pages/Reducing-greenhouse-gas-emissions-from-ships.aspx#:~:text=In%202018%2C%20IMO%20adopted%20an,out%20as%20soon%20as%20possible
8 http://www.blaainno.dk/
9 https://ourworldindata.org/transport

9
REVERSE SUPPLY CHAINS

One issue with linear supply chains described in previous chapters is the creation of waste. Waste has become a big problem as it affects the environment and social structure of many communities. The Box "Note: What happens to unwanted clothes in fast fashion?" describes the problems arising from waste streams that overwhelm a community and the potentials for solving this. Much of our waste has direct adversarial environmental effects. For example, it is estimated that 8 million tonnes of waste enter the world's oceans each year.[1] In 2012, we produced a worldwide total of 50 million tons of electronic waste. The problem is projected to increase further. Specifically, municipal solid waste is expected to increase by about 70% is expected by 2050.[2] Factors such as population growth, urbanisation and economic growth, as well as consumer shopping habits, play a vital role in this prediction.

Note: What happens to unwanted clothes in fast fashion?

Countries in West Africa are drowning from the 15 million used clothes shipped there every week. The waste is earmarked for reuse or recycling but quality issues that it can often only be placed in landfill. Many of the fast fashion items arriving are damaged or even falling apart. These items end up in the already overflowing landfills making up an estimated 40% of what is shipped. Clothing is not biodegradable and can hence not be placed in municipal landfills. The landfills are often not safe, and items end up being washed into the sea. There, they affect sea life. In other cases, fashion waste is burned polluting local air or buried and polluting the soil. These problems add to the environmental and social issues created in the production of fast fashion, including extensive water use, poverty of workers and child labour.

The problem is increasing in magnitude. Western consumers now buy on average 60% more clothing than 15 years ago. Global clothing production doubled between 2000 and 2014. Globally, fashion waste accounts to about $500 billion. Landfills in

---

DOI: 10.4324/9781003345077-14

other countries, including Chile, are similarly overwhelmed with the amount of fashion waste dumped here. 39,000 tonnes of used clothing that cannot be sold end up in landfill here.

Many attempts at reusing or recycling some of this fashion waste exist. For example, the Ecotex Group specialises in reusing and recycling used clothing and producing items, such as ecologic yarns and fabrics. Another example, EcoFibra created thermal insulation from the fashion waste in the Tarapacá region in Chile. The insulation product come in the form of blankets and plates or in bulk with different degrees of density, thickness and insulating capacity. They are used in the construction of new housing as well as renovations.

The UN and other organisations now work to have producers of these fast fashion items commit to taking responsibility for the end-of-life of these items. The Extended Producer Responsibility (EPR) is an environmental policy extending producers' responsibility to the entire life cycle of the product they place on the market to include waste collection and other reverse supply chain steps. The policy extends across product types and currently includes packaging and user electronics.

Source: https://www.bbc.co.uk/news/world-africa-58836618;
https://www.aljazeera.com/gallery/2021/11/8/chiles-
desert-dumping-ground-for-fast-fashion-leftovers; http://
ecofibrachile.cl/product.html; https://ecotexgroup.com/production-
and-services/; https://www.forbes.com/sites/quora/2017/07/26/
fast-fashion-is-a-disaster-for-women-and-the-environment/?sh=164219b81fa4

As a result, many legislators have introduced policies to force take-back of products at the end of their use phases. For example, EPR aims to hold producers physically and financially responsible for collecting and treating their products environmentally responsible at the end of their useful life. This take-back legislation applies to, for example, packaging, automobiles and appliances. Especially in the electronics industry, this take-back mentality has been included in many national frameworks across the globe. For example, the Waste Electrical and Electronic Equipment (WEEE) Directive by the EU requires producers to be financially and physically responsible for the recovery of e-waste and defines a collection *rate* target of 65%. Similarly, Japan has implemented Specified Household Appliance Recycling (SHAR) and Brazil the National Solid Waste Policy (NSWP). For companies operating in these sectors, reverse supply chain management is a reality.

Reverse supply chains essentially move materials, parts and goods from downstream partners to upstream ones. As such, reverse supply chain management is concerned with the "design, plan, and control the reverse supply chains that process returned products from the customer, recover their value, and use or sell them again" (Blackburn et al., 2004, p. 6). Reverse supply chains can enable better use of resources and can open up new markets, with related sustainability benefits. Reverse supply chain management often also includes the option to dispose of the retrieved product (material or part). For the purpose of this chapter, we focus on retrieving the value of the product and ignore disposal for now. Reverse supply chains focus on the activities depicted in Figure 9.1, namely reuse, remanufacture and recycling. The process starts with reverse logistics to enable product (part, material, etc.) collection.

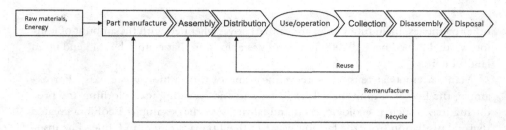

FIGURE 9.1 Reverse supply chain loops.

Product collection and reverse logistics

Reverse logistics concerns the processes for sending returned products to back up the supply chain for resale, repair, reuse, remanufacture, recycling or disposal. The aim is often to avoid or limit burning or burying of returned products and strive for reuse. This is especially relevant when components or materials have longer life cycles than the products they are part of. Reverse logistics can be a necessity due to legal or regulatory obligations (e.g., product warranty) or compliance with voluntary certification. Reverse logistics can also offer companies' advantages and possibilities, including the possibility of achieving economic, strategic, reputational and relational advantages. Finally, ethical choices rooted in socially responsible behaviour can inspire strategies of reverse logistics. Reasons to implement reverse logistics include the following[3]:

- *Consumer return:* Consumer may return products that they discovered to have defects. This includes requests for replacement covered by warranty, repairs and so on. This applies especially in e-commerce channels as many countries define a right to return goods.
- *Marketing or distribution return:* If a company withdraws a product from market (because it is phased out, a substitute product is launched), the marketing and sales department imposes product returns. Similarly, a product may need to be reallocated between nodes along the distribution network, requiring product collection.
- *Asset return:* Products may need to be returned at the end of their use. In Business-to-Business (B2B) contexts, for example, IT equipment, industrial equipment, quarry machinery, reusable containers, racks, etc., are collected to be re-introduced into the distribution cycle, recycled or disposed of safely.
- *Product or manufacturing recall*: In special circumstances products may need to be recalled because of faults. This can concern, for example, safety issues for the user or the case of serious quality problems, restrictions of the use of materials or components imposed by regulatory bodies.
- *Environmental return:* Different regulations now require companies to take their products back after use. An example is the EU regulation regarding waste from electrical and electronic equipment (WEEE).[4] This aims to recover products, components and materials based on the value associated with the different recovery options.

There are obvious differences between the management of the forward flow, which makes the product available to the consumer, and the management of the reverse flow, which aims to recover the residual value of the product at the end of its life cycle. Reverse flows are characterised as follows[5]:

- High levels of uncertainty regarding:
  - Quality and conditions of the returned product.
  - Quantity, resulting in a lower forecast reliability.
  - Timing of the backward flows, strongly influenced by the final consumer, as a starting point of the process.
- Dependence on consumer behaviour creating uncertainty regarding the willingness of the final consumer to:
  - Return the product rather than adding it to the (often more convenient) waste stream.
  - Buy products that are used, remanufactured or recovered rather than new ones.
  - Willingness to cooperate in the recovery process.
- Operational complexity resulting from:
  - The number, location and accessibility of collection points.
  - The cost-effectiveness of the recovery process. This is affected by product inspection and sorting, which are in general labour intensive.

Table 9.1 provides a summary of some of the main concerns, comparison forward and reverse logistics.

With aim to recapture value, management consideration focuses on the ability to disassemble the product, components or packaging in return flows. Here, the characteristics of the returned products can create significant managerial challenges as follows[6]:

- *Product composition* concerns the number and variety of components and materials used in product. Uncertainty regarding the intrinsic characteristics of used materials, the utilisation of multi-material components or "monstrous hybrids" composed of hazardous and non-polluting components can create difficulties in the disassembly and sorting processes. This determines the costs and tie of these processes and often even limits the feasibility of different recovery options. This is an issue many manufacturing

TABLE 9.1 Challenges of reverse logistics in comparison to forward logistics[a]

	Forward logistics	Reverse logistics
Forecasting	Depending on product demand	Depending on the supply of used products
Product quality	Uniform product quality with uniform packaging	Not uniform with potential damages in the product itself and its packaging
Pricing	Relatively uniform based on consistent logistic flows with easily visible distribution costs	Dependent on many factors, including product condition and accessibility of collection points with less directly visible distribution costs
Speed	Often very important	Often not a priority
Inventory management	Consistent	Not consistent

a Based on, for example, Heizer, J., Render, B., Munson, C. (2020). *Operations Management: Sustainability and Supply Chain Management*, 13th ed Pearson, p. 492.

companies need to address first, as it concerns product design (see Chapter 2). One solution is the use of modular designs.

- *Deterioration* concerns the residual functional capacity of the returned product or part. These can vary substantially as returns can consist of barely used items as well as products that have been used to the point of breaking. The condition of returned products affect in how far residual value can be captured through, for example, reuse. Deterioration is connected to usage but also to technological obsolescence, economic obsolescence or the unprofitability in trade-off between its replacement with a new product and its re-entry on the market.
- *Use Pattern* concerns the location, intensity and duration of use. Location includes the dispersion of users and the positioning of collection points. Intensity of use is connected to deterioration and drives the reverse supply route (reuse, remanufacture and recycle) of the specific product. Duration of use is often (but not always) proportional to its intensity. Use patterns affect the effectiveness and efficiency of reverse flow processes, especially in terms of entering the product into reverse flows.

To manage reverse flows typically involves the following steps[7]:

- *Gatekeeping* refers to the decision-making on whether to direct a product, part or component into the reverse supply chain.
- *Collection* to group the products, parts or components directed for the reverse supply chain and transferring them to the point of recovery.
- *Inspection or testing* to ascertain the condition of the returned product, part or component. This can include visual, functional and diagnostic testing.
- *Sortation or selection* to separate products, parts or components by type and allocate recovery option.
- *Disposition* to transfer the product, part or component to its destination for potential further processing.
- *Recovery* to obtain any residual value and assess best available option for potential further processing.

One of the main challenges for managers of reverse supply chains of consumer products is often the possibility to collect products. An example of how this was overcome is presented in the Box "Example: EcoATM."

Example: EcoATM

EcoATM offers a collection service for consumers to sell the used small electronics equipment that they no longer needed. Starting in 2011, EcoATM installed kiosks at US malls and other retail locations where consumers could return their used phones, tablets and MP3 players and instantly receive cash into the reverse supply chain cycle. By September 2014, the company had installed 1,100 kiosks around the United States of America. The kiosk uses machine vision and machine learning algorithms to determine the device's model and condition and instantly match the phone with an industry buyer, who already agreed to a price (determined via pre-auction of the highest bidder). EcoATM screens buyers for proper disposal practices and for being "good business partners." The company holds on to devices for 30 days in case they were stolen. Similar services are provided by other companies such as ReCellular.

Source: https://www.ecoatm.com/

Reuse

Product reuse refers to the re-entry of a product into the secondary market, where the product is used for the same purpose for which they were originally designed and produced. This may include resale of the item. Reuse requires redistribution after collection and testing. It can require product reconditioning, including simple inspection and cleaning. It can, however, also happen without any reconditioning of the product. Product reuse often becomes relevant for:

- Returns due to overstock (e.g., clothing or furnishing industries), which can be sold as new.
- Existence of a secondary market (e.g., books, cars and DVDs) often for charities.
- Low-value items related to, for example, product packaging.

Product reuse has an obvious positive performance effect regarding environmental sustainability. Linking back to the example of LCA for shopping bags, the Box "Tool: LCA of shopping bags – Determining the need for reuse."

Tool: LCA of shopping bags – Determining the need for reuse

In their LCA of commonly used shopping bags, the UK Environment Agency compared the following four bags: a lightweight carrier made from high-density polyethylene (HDPE), a "bag for life" made from low-density polyethylene (LDPE), a paper bag, a heavier plastic bag with stiffening inserts made from non-woven polypropylene (PP), and a cotton bag. Based on the LCA of each type of carrier bag, the study concluded that the predominant environmental impact was created through resource use and production. In comparison, environmental impacts created through transport, secondary packaging and end-of-life management had a minimal influence. One of the key take-aways was the need to reuse bags as many times as possible. This can include primary reuse (i.e., for the originally intended purpose) and secondary reuse (i.e., for other purposes, including as bin liners). Reuse provides greater environmental benefits than other reverse supply chain activities, such as recycling.

Based on the LCA of each carrier bag, the analysts calculated the number of times each type of bag needs to be reused to "break even" with the environmental impact of a HDPE bag, which was commonly used for supermarket shopping in the United Kingdom during the 2000s. They used different scenarios for reusing the HDPE bags as a baseline to compare required number of reuses for the other carrier bags. These scenarios were:

- No reuse.
- 40.3% of HDPE bags are reused as bin liners.

- 100% of HDPE bags are reused as bin liners.
- HDPE bags are used three times.

Based on these four scenarios, the analysts calculated how many times each of the other carrier bags would need to be reused. The results are displayed in the table below. The results show the partly extensive reuse needed from some of the carrier bags to outweigh the environmental impacts of their production. Specific statistics on how often these carrier bags are reused in practice give, however, different indications. For example, studies on paper bags show no evidence that consumers reuse them.

	No reuse	40.3% reuse of HDPE bag	100% reuse of HDPE bag	HDPE bag used three times
Paper bag	3	4	7	9
LDPE bag	4	5	9	12
PP bag	11	14	26	33
Cotton bag	131	173	327	393

The report, however, ignores the effects of littering, the ability and willingness of consumers to change behaviour, any adverse impacts of degradable polymers in the recycling stream and the potential economic impacts on UK business.

Source: Edwards, C., Fry, J.M. (2011). Life cycle assessment of supermarket carrier bags: A review of the bags available in 2006. Bristol, UK. https://assets. publishing.service.gov.uk/government/uploads/system/uploads/attachment_ data/file/291023/scho0711buan-e-e.pdf

Reuse of tools, equipment and packaging offers not only cost-based advantages but also opportunities to integrating business operations closer with suppliers' processes and the wider community. One example is described in the Box "Example: SIA."

Example: SIA

Subaru of Indiana Automotive, Inc. (SIA) receives truckloads of wheels, which are secured by small temporary brass lug nuts. SIA used to discard them, amounting to 33,000 pounds wasted per year. Then, they started collecting them and returning them to their wheel supplier for reuse until they are no longer serviceable. At this stage, these brass lug nuts are recycled for the brass material. Similarly, SIA also reuses the Styrofoam forms, which are used to cushion delicate components on their trip from Japan to Indiana. They now return these forms to their supplier in Japan, who reuses them in future trips. After five uses, they end up in Japan, where they are recycled (85% of it is). Overall, these practices reduce the number of consumables in the system.

Source: Sheffi, Y., Blanco, E. (2018). *Balancing Green: When to Embrace Sustainability in a Business (and When Not To)*. MIT Press, Chapter 7.

Remanufacture

Remanufacturing refers to the process of restoring a used product to a common aesthetic and operating standard. This includes disassembly, cleaning, reworking, reassembly and testing, and hence involves potentially costly and complex actions. For example, disassembly and reassembly are labour-intensive regardless of the product or industry. Similarly, cleaning is labour-intensive for most industries. Reworking is both labour- and capital-intensive. This means that remanufacturing usually focuses on products, whose recovery potential is associated with an increase in value. Remanufacturing is also often described using other terms, such as "refurbish," "rebuild," "recondition," "overhaul" and "restore." Because of this breadth of terminology used, it is difficult to pinpoint the largest remanufacturing industry, includes reconditioning, refining, retreating and refurbish.

The goal of remanufacturing is to restore the product to the same state as the new product in terms of functionality and aesthetic. Sometimes the performance of a remanufactured product can even be higher, for example, if original components are replaced with more recent components. Here, product design principles (see Chapter 2, e.g., design for disassembly) can support these functions and hence increase business case for remanufacturing.

Remanufacturing offers different advantages and disadvantages to the manufacturing firm, providing potential motivations and barriers to include remanufacturing operations. Table 9.2 lists some of these in an overview. Because of some of the disadvantages, many Original Equipment Manufacturers (OEMs) sell their remanufactured products through different channels than their new products. For example, remanufactured computers by Hewlett-Packard (HP) are not available through retailers, such as Best Buy, but need to be purchased using HP's online outlet store.

TABLE 9.2 Advantages and disadvantages of remanufacturing[a]

Advantages	Disadvantages
Extended market with potential to target new customers	Consumers' lower willingness-to-pay for remanufactured products ranging from −15% to −50% depending on the product. The Box "Consumer's willingness to pay for remanufactured products" for more detail
Ability to tap into green segment of customers. This concerns consumers that prefer a remanufactured product to a new one if they are in the same price range	
	Potential lower durability of remanufactured products
Undercut competition from cheaper, non-brand name imports. For example, in the power tool industry	Cannibalisation effect: customers who are willing to buy a (higher margin) new product buy a (lower priced remanufactured product
Increase resource efficiency	Responsibility of warranty or guarantee is not clear
Increase potential product use cycles through integrating remanufacturing strategies into the product design phases	Uncertainty in reverse logistics can limit the possibility of cost-efficient design
	Dependence on downstream partners for access to products

a   Based on Souza, G.C. (2017). *Sustainable Operations and Closed Loop Supply Chains*. Business Expert Press; 2nd ed., Chapter 7; Boorsma, N., Peck, D., Bakker, T., Bakker, C., Balkenende, R. (2022). The strategic value of design for remanufacturing: A case study of professional imaging equipment. *Journal of Remanufacturing*. Doi: 10.1007/s13243-021-00107-0.

Note: Consumer's willingness to pay for remanufactured products

Researchers have conducted various experiments to determine the consumers' willingness to pay for remanufactured products, consistently proofing that realised prices are substantially below those of new products. In one experiment, researchers auctioned identical new and remanufactured power tools on eBay and identical new and remanufactured Internet routers on eBay business. The remanufactured and new products had identical manufacturer warranties and functionalities. The researchers assessed the winning bid, which provides a measure of a consumer's willingness-to-pay. For the remanufactured product, the winning bid was on average 15% lower than the winning bid for the new product.

In another study, researchers found an even higher difference for different consumer electronic products auctioned on eBay. The average price discounts for remanufactured products relative to new products ranged between 15% for some consumer electronics and 40% for video-game consoles. In this study, again, the warranty and product characteristics were comparable between new and remanufactured products, meaning that the auctioned price can be attributed to the remanufactured nature of the products.

Finally, a large survey by the United States International Trade Commission (USITC) studied American remanufacturers in diverse industries, such as compressors, automotive parts, office furniture, electrical motors and industrial machinery. The survey finds that remanufactured products are sold at a 30%–50% discount relative to comparable new products.

Source: Guide, Jr. V.D., Li, K. (2010). Market cannibalization of new product sales by remanufactured products. *Decision Sciences,* vol. 41, no. 3, pp. 547–572; Subramanian, R., Subramanyam, R. (2012). Key factors in the market for remanufactured products: Empirical evidence from eBay. *Manufacturing & Service Operations Management*, vol. 14, no. 2, pp. 315–326.

Remanufacturing examples exist in industry, and one long-standing such example is described in Box "Example: Cat Reman."

Example: Cat Reman

Since 1973, Caterpillar, Inc. (Cat) provides remanufactured products called Cat Reman. Cat Reman is based on exchange system where the customer returns used components in exchange for a remanufactured product. When the product or component is returned to a Cat dealer, Cat Reman salvages, re-engineers and remanufactures it using state-of-the-art processes and technologies. Through this, the manufacturer of construction and mining equipment recapture and renew the built-in quality and performance of their products and components. The prices are on average 40% lower than equivalent new products or components. This means that Cat Reman lowers the operating costs for their customer, reduces material waste and creates less need for raw material to make new products.

The manufacturer offers more than 7,600 Cat Reman products, which it markets as genuine Cat replacement products with the same exacting specifications as new products. In addition, Cat incorporates the latest engineering updates. In one-year period, they have processed 2.1 million end-of-life units, which account for more than 130 million pounds of material from recycled iron.

Sources: https://www.caterpillar.com/en/brands/cat-reman.html;
https://testmec-op.weebly.com/reman-parts.html

Recycling

Recycling refers to the process of converting materials from products in waste streams into new materials, product parts or products. It involves looping back to deeper supply chain tiers that handle raw materials. To recycle (parts of) a product, product parts need to be separated, collected and processed, with recycled materials being remarketed and re-integrated into new supply chains. Recycling requires collection, disassembly and separation of materials and components into similar types. In some industry sectors, such as fashion, recycling required shredding of the product. The Box "Note: Recycling definitions" offers an overview of the different terms used to refer to different aspects of recycling.

Note: Recycling definitions

Based on recycling plastic, the following definitions of different methods of recycling can be differentiated:

Primary recycling (or closed-loop recycling) refers to the mechanical reprocessing of the material into a new product with equivalent properties.

Upcycling: The new product retains or improves the properties of the material.

Downcycling (or secondary recycling, downgrading) refers to the mechanical reprocessing of the material into products with lower properties. The resulting new product is often of low value.

Tertiary recycling (or chemical or feedstock recycling) refers to the recovery of a material's chemical constituents and involves the structural breakdown of materials into their original raw core components and subsequent buildup of material with properties equivalent to the original material.

Source: Bocken, N.M.P., de Pauw, I., Bakker, C., van der Grinten, B. (2016). Product design and business model strategies for a circular economy. *Journal of Industrial and Production Engineering*, vol. 33, no. 5, pp. 308–320. https://doi.org/10.1080/21681015.2016.1172124

TABLE 9.3 Advantages and disadvantages of recycling[a]

Advantages	Disadvantages
Reduce waste, especially toxic waste	Recyclability is often dependent on the value of raw material and the cost of recycling in comparison to reuse
Reduce demand on raw materials or new materials	Require reverse logistics with related barriers (see above) and often require the collaboration of additional supply chain members
Can create a source of additional or new business	Net effects on GHG emissions may sometimes be increased through activities of, for example, downcycling or upcycling
	Potential quality impacts of recycling

a Based on Souza, G.C. (2017). *Sustainable Operations and Closed Loop Supply Chains.* Business Expert Press; 2nd ed., Chapter 7.

Recycling offers different advantages and disadvantages as listed in Table 9.3. The result, especially of some of the disadvantages, is that in practice, many materials or products remain not recyclable. This has led policy makers to take a harsher stance on what products may display the recycling symbol as described in the Box "Note: Use of the recycling symbol."

Note: Use of the recycling symbol

Policy makers have realised that products, which display the three-arrow symbol for recycling, are not necessarily recyclable. As a result, they start introducing bills and guidelines that ban companies from using the symbol if their product is indeed not recyclable. An example is the US state of California, which passed a related bill in September 2021. This bill requires companies that wish to display the recycling symbol on their products to prove that the material is indeed recycled in most Californian communities. In addition, they need to prove that the recycled material is used to make new products. Before the bill was introduced, any product could have the recycling symbol irrespective of its recyclability. This could mislead consumers into thinking that waste is recycled when indeed it is not.

Source: www.nytimes.com/2021/09/08/climate/arrows-recycling-symbol-california.amp.html, September 2021.

Examples of supply chains based on recycling are manifold. Some of these require additional supply chain partners, such as the example presented in the Box "Example 1: Terracycle." In other cases, the recycling is directed by the focal company, who produced or manufactured the product. The Boxes "Example 2: Nike ReUSE A SHOE" and "Example 3: Johnson Controls" describe these in more detail.

Example 1: Terracycle

"We focus on making things recyclable that are not recyclable" is the motto of the company Terracycle. Focusing on the issue of collecting products at the end of their primary use cycle, many products do not enter the reverse supply chain because the cost of collecting and processing the products exceeds the value retained in the resulting glass. While in practice, many consumer products can be recycled technically, they are often not recycled in practice because it costs more to collect and process the item than it is worth. This is where Terracycle enters the chain.

Terracycle partners with companies to open the recycling cycle up for the product streams. With this approach, they have achieved great success. One example is the recycling of cigarette butts. Cigarette butts take between 18 months and 10 years to break down, creating a lasting littering problem in many communities. Partnering with tobacco companies, such as Santa Fe Natural Tobacco Company, Terracycle funds a programme of waste collection and recycling. The waste collected through this programme is recycled into a variety of industrial products, such as plastic pallets, and tobacco as compost.

A second example is the recycling of stationary, including writing instruments, glue sticks, watercolour dispensers, paint sets and flexible packaging. For this programme, Terracycle partnered with BIC, the French manufacturer of disposable consumer products, such as pens or lighters. This programme enables consumers to request recycling online, collect their items and send them to the recycling station. It also includes an in-store version to encourage consumers to bring used items back for recycling and hence increases foot traffic in the stores.

Coincidentally, at Terracycle social equality is practised, too. For example, their chief executive officer (CEO) earns only seven times as much as the lowest paid employee – on average this is a factor of 303.

Source: https://www.terracycle.com/en-US/brigades/bic

Example 2: Nike ReUSE A SHOE

Nike collects used and unusable sport shoes in their stores and combines them together with scrap material from the shoe making process to give them new life. Starting in 1993, the Nike ReUSE A SHOE programme initially downcycled the materials from their sport shoes to become NikeGrind material. The manufacturer of sport apparel cuts each returned shoe into three slices containing (i) the rubber outsole, (ii) the foam midsole and (iii) the fibre upper. Each slice is fed through grinders and purified. In the end, the following three high-quality materials are the result:

- Nike Grind Rubber: As the result from the shoe's outsole, this material is often downcycled for track surfaces, interlocking gym flooring tiles and playground surfacing. More recently, Nike also recycles this material into new Nike products using it for outsoles of new trainers, such as the Nike Pegasus or the Jordan XX3.
- Nike Grind Foam: As the result from the shoe's midsole, this material is downcycled into cushioning for outdoor basketball and tennis courts, and futsal fields.
- Nike Grind Fibre: Stemming from the shoe's fabric upper, this material is used in the creation of cushioning pads for facilities like indoor synthetic courts and wood courts.

More recently, Nike also produces the "Trash Talk" shoe from recycled material. The "Trash Talk" shoe, a professional-quality basketball shoe made from recycled materials, is constructed from recycled scraps of leather and synthetic materials and has a sole made from recycled rubber. The product design is strong enough for a professional athletes.

Source: https://www.nike.com/dk/en/help/a/recycle-shoes; https://recyclenation.com/2012/08/nike-reuse-shoe-program/; https://recyclenation.com/2009/09/nike-trashy-shoes-recycled-scraps/

Example 3: Johnson Controls

Johnson Controls International Plc. (known in Europe as ecosteps) is the world's largest supplier of automotive batteries and have been recycling batteries since 1904. By 2015, they recycled more than 97% of the batteries they sold in North America. From each sold battery, they can effectively recover 99% of materials and make new lead-acid batteries containing 80% recycled materials. For this purpose they developed close ties with retailers, auto shops and junkyards to obtain a constant supply of waste batteries. By now, their reverse logistics operations are built to optimise the collection of old batteries every time they deliver new ones. They recycle lead and other materials of the battery, including the plastic housing to make new housings. Johnson Controls also recycle the acidic liquid electrolytes inside the battery and reuse them in new batteries or supply them to makers of detergents and glass.

Because they source 80%–90% of their lead from recycled batteries, Johnson Controls can:

- Reduce their dependence on volatile markets where lead prices fluctuate as much as $500–$4000
- Rely on domestic supply of lead and hence reduce their dependence on foreign lead producer situated in countries, such as China, Australia and Peru. This also means that they decrease their dependence on exchange rate volatilities.

Source: Sheffi, Y., Blanco, E. (2018). *Balancing Green: When to Embrace Sustainability in a Business (and When Not To)*. MIT Press, Chapter 7.

Closed-loop supply chains

Closed–loop supply chains require a proactive approach of supply chain management to optimise all forward and reverse flows. This often involves preparing for returns prior to product introduction. Companies need to design and implement end–of–life systems for the physical return of products that facilitate reuse, remanufacturing or recycle. The purpose is to extend sustainability performance across all three dimensions. To successfully design closed–loop supply chains, companies need to consider factors, including number and location of facilities for collecting and storing forward and reverse product flows (including their capacity and channels), supplier selection and sourcing strategies. An example of a closed-loop supply chain is presented in the Box "Example: **Dell and Goodwill Industries**."

Example: Dell and Goodwill Industries

In collaboration, Dell and Goodwill Industries have set up a reverse supply chain enabling them to avoid 2 billion pounds of electronic waste and re-introduce it at different nodes in the supply chain. Goodwill Industries is a US charity, which collects and resells lightly used merchandise through their 2,000 outlets. Dell partnered with them because they lacked their own network of retail outlets, limiting their ability to take back used products and e-waste. Through the partnership with Goodwill, consumers can drop off their used computers and other technology products (even non-Dell) at Goodwill's donation sites around the United States of America and hence enter it into the reverse supply chain.

Once the equipment is in the reverse supply stream, three things can happen. First, Goodwill reconditions and resells newer devices with remaining life span for reuse. Second, the returned computers are disassembled, and the parts resold for reuse. Here, the modular nature of computers enables disassembly into its parts, such as memory, storage and peripheral cards. Third, any otherwise unusable items or parts are carefully recycled by Dell.

Through this set-up, Dell had recycled 1.42 billion pounds of electronic waste by 2015. In 2019 alone, they recovered 2 billion pounds. Dell and Goodwill not only help the environment by avoiding unnecessary waste and reducing the amount of new materials needed for producing new computers, but they also address social responsibility goals. Goodwill help people with disabilities by providing training in refurbishing PCs and enabling them to work with technology.

The partnership with Goodwill provides Dell also with a supply of recyclable plastic. In their programme Dell Reconnect, the computer manufacturer separates, sorts and inspects the plastic coming from electronics collected at Goodwill locations and then ships bales of certain types of recyclable plastic to its supplier, Wistron Corporation. Wistron, who is based in Taiwan, shreds the return stream and blends it with virgin plastic to achieve the required structural integrity needed for new computers. In 2015, the mix had 35% of recycled plastic. Then Wistron moulds the plastic into new parts for Dell computers.

By the end of 2015, Dell reported that 16 models of displays and three models of desktops were made with closed-loop recycled plastic. By 2019, this had increased to 125 models. Through this set-up, Dell creates 11% lower carbon emissions compared to using virgin plastics.

Source: Sheffi, Y., Blanco, E. (2018) *Balancing Green: When to Embrace Sustainability in a Business (and When Not To)*. MIT Press, Chapter 7; https://corporate.delltechnologies.com/en-us/social-impact/advancing-sustainability/how-to-recycle.htm#/; https://www.yourgoodwill.org/donate/where-how/computers-dell-reconnect; https://corporate.delltechnologies.com/content/dam/delltechnologies/assets/corporate/pdf/progress-made-real-reports/dell-fy19-csr-report.pdf

Connecting back to the opening example of this chapter, reverse supply chain concerns of material recycling or reuse have also been considered to solve some of the challenges in the fashion industry. An example is described in the Box "Note: Closed loop fashion."

Note: Closed loop fashion

Many retail firms in the fashion industry offer their own entry points for used apparel into the reverse supply chains. Rapanui, for example, offer a circular line of clothing where consumers can send their worn-out garments back directly to them. The aim is to increase the availability to materials of sufficiently high quality for reuse and recycling.

Textile production is a major polluting industry. The combined GHG emissions from textile production in 2015 totalled 1.2 billion tonnes of CO_2 equivalent. This represents 10% of global carbon emissions and is higher than the emissions from international air and sea transport combined. Production (including farming) of natural materials, such as cotton, is highly water intense. Textile production requires about 93 billion cubic meters of water annually. In addition, much of the production process results in polluted water streams with hazardous chemicals being discharged into the local environments, which often already suffer from water scarcity.

Using recycled materials in new clothing is a new trend among retailer s and producers. *The Guardian* reports that more than 70 brands, among whom are H&M, Madewell, J Crew and Nike, have committed to increasing the share of recycled polyester alone in their new clothing. Despite these commitments, currently less than 1% of clothes are currently recycled into new fibres.

Recycling materials of garments may, however, only be a partial solution to the environmental problem of the fashion industry. For example, using recycled polyester instead of the virgin equivalent could reduce emissions by up to 32%. Instead, it is a step in the direction of reducing environmental impacts of the fashion industry. Using recycled synthetics, for example, does not solve the problem of microplastics, which shed from garments during washing and use and often end up in water ways.

In addition, there is the risk of a backlash effect, where garment producers are inclined to use more fabrics based on plastics. This in turn would reduce environmental impacts during production but increase environmental effects during use of the garment, where microplastics end up in sewage water through washing etc. The UK House of Commons Environmental Audit Committee hence demands "Fashion that saves resources and energy, minimises plastic pollution, reduces waste and thrives" (p. 50).

Sources: https://rapanuiclothing.com/; https://www.theguardian.com/environment/2021/nov/06/clothes-made-from-recycled-materials-sustainable-plastic-climate; https://www.forbes.com/sites/quora/2017/07/26/fast-fashion-is-a-disaster-for-women-and-the-environment/?sh=164219b-81fa4; "A new textiles economy: Redesigining fashion's future" (2017), Report by Ellen MacArthur Foundation; https://www-bbc-co-uk.cdn.ampproject.org/c/s/www.bbc.co.uk/news/entertainment-arts-58515849.amp; https://publications.parliament.uk/pa/cm201719/cmselect/cmenvaud/1952/full-report.html#heading-8

Notes

1 https://ourworldindata.org/#entries
2 https://www.statista.com/statistics/916625/global-generation-of-municipal-solid-waste-forecast/; in contrast, overall waste generation in the EU is reported to be stable in the EU COM 571 report.
3 Based on Belvedere, V., Grando, A. (2017). *Sustainable Operations and Supply Chain Management*, Wiley, Chapter 7; https://supplychaingamechanger.com/the-reverse-logistics-role-in-supply-chain-trends/
4 https://ec.europa.eu/environment/topics/waste-and-recycling/waste-electrical-and-electronic-equipment-weee_en
5 Based on: Belvedere, V., Grando, A. (2017). *Sustainable Operations and Supply Chain Management*. Wiley, Chapter 7; Grant, D.B., Trautrims, A., Wong, C.Y. (2013). *Sustainable Logistics and Supply Chain Management*. London, Koganpage, p. 19.
6 De Brito, M.P., Dekker, R. (2010). A framework for reverse logistics. In: Dekker, R., Fleishmann, M., Inderfurth, K., Van Wassenhove, L.N. *Reverse Logistics: Quantitative Methods for Closed-loop Supply Chains*. Springer, pp. 3–27.
7 Rogers, D.S., Tibben-Lembke, R.S. (2001). An examination of reverse logistics practices. *Journal of Business Logistics*, vol. 22, no. 2, pp. 129–148.

10

CIRCULAR ECONOMY

Reverse supply chains offer the possibility of reducing waste that leaves the production use system. However, most of todays' waste still ends up in landfill or incineration. Worldwide, less than 20% of (solid municipal) waste is recycled each year while 44% of waste globally go to landfill (34% were recycled or composted).[1] The European Union (EU) reports that only 40% of the solid waste is reused or recycled while the remaining 60% go to landfill or incineration. This rate, however, differs highly across countries as some EU member states have a recycling rate of more than 80%.[2] This shows the geographic differences in using waste as an input resource.

But it is not only physical waste that creates problems. For example, The Ellen MacArthur foundation reports that an average car remains parked 92% of the time and even when it is moving, it only carries on average 1.5 people at a time.[3] Similarly, 46% of fruits and vegetables are lost or wasted in the EU. This structural waste exists across many sectors regarding the products and services we use. In other words, many of our products (and services) are underutilised in comparison to the capacity they offer. There is hence a big potential to create sustainability performance by addressing shortcomings of existing systems through introducing circular economy.

What is a circular economy?

The circular economy is defined as "the economy that provides multiple value-creation mechanisms which are decoupled from the consumption of finite resources."[4] Circular economy is inspired by the biological sphere, where waste becomes an integral resource for another process, without the depletion of energy or other resources. This definition of circular economy reflects the differences to a linear economy and goes beyond the reverse flow of material and resources. At the centre of creating circular economy is the value loss currently inherent in forward and reverse supply chains. As such, it goes beyond resource efficiency and instead, "A circular economy seeks to rebuild capital, whether this is financial, manufactured, human, social or natural. This ensures enhanced flows of goods and services" (Ellen MacArthur Foundation).

DOI: 10.4324/9781003345077-15

Circular economy is based upon three main principles[5]:

- Balance resource flows to preserve and enhance natural capital. This can require the use of renewable resources in production, such as renewable energy sources. It can also be achieved through returning nutrients to ecosystems.
- Increase utility of product, components and materials to increase or optimise resource yields. This can include increasing utility rates of individual products or parts in use as well as circulating products, components and materials through closed-loop supply chains.
- Enable system effectiveness by reducing and eliminating detrimental effects to the environment and society, including water, solid, noise pollution or detrimental health effects.

Through creating a circular economy, the Ellen MacArthur Foundation estimates the potential to save $700 million in material costs, to create 48% reduction in CO_2 emissions and to reduce $550 billion in healthcare costs associated with the food sector. In addition, circular economy can increase the disposable income for EU households by €3000 per year and reduce 47% of traffic congestion in China's cities. These are a selection of potential benefits from establishing circular economy.

A much-simplified representation of circular economy is depicted in Figure 10.1. It shows significant differences to the figure at the beginning of the chapter on reverse supply chains:

- A perfect closed loop requires no addition of raw materials or other inputs for production. This is represented by showing "renewable inputs" into the technical system.
- A circular economy creates no waste or pollution. As such, the waste stream is eliminated from Figure 10.1 (in comparison to Figure 9.1 from Chapter 9).
- Within the system, material streams extend beyond the reverse supply chain activities of reuse, remanufacture and recycle. Additional steps are often summarised in the 10R principle (resell, reuse, recondition, refine, retreat, recover, repair, refurbish, remanufacture and recycle) and can include other activities, such as donations.[6]

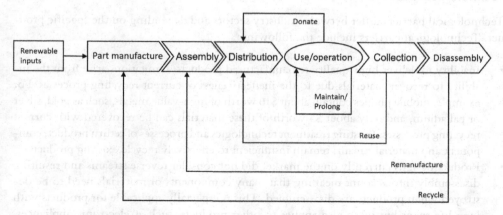

FIGURE 10.1 Figurative and simplified representation of circular economy.

The power of circular economy

The loops in Figure 10.1 show the possible lengthening of the life cycle of products. Products, components and materials cycle back endlessly to suppliers, manufacturers and the next generation of consumers. This gives the circular economy power to achieve sustainability performance as follows[7]:

The power of the inner circle: Maximising the use(fulness) of a product, component or material enables minimising material usage in comparison to linear production system. The objective is to tighten the inner circle by requiring fewer and less changes to a product to enable it to return faster to use. The fewer steps needed when looping the product, component or material back into reuse or remanufacturing, the higher the potential savings on the shares of material, labour, energy and capital embedded in the product and hence the lower externalities of its production.

The power of circling longer: Maximising the number of consecutive cycles and the time each product, component or material spends within each cycle prolongs the product use and ultimately maximises the relative contribution of the shares of material, labour, energy and capital embedded in the product.

The power of cascaded use: Enabling cascaded (re)use of a product, component or material through primary, secondary, etc., reuse maximises its value in terms of usefulness and enables the reduction of virgin materials in the value chain. Each time a flow of raw or virgin materials is being replaced with a reused one, and the pressure on system inputs is eased and reduced.

The power of pure circles: By utilising uncontaminated materials in products, collection and redistribution into closed-loop supply chains are simplified and enable maintaining of the material quality and value. This in turn increases material productivity and product longevity.

Current barriers

There remain various barriers to achieving circular economy. These barriers even apply to supply chains that effectively implemented closed-loop supply chains. These barriers can be summarised as technological, market and economic, regulatory, supply chain and cultural.[8]

Technological barriers

Technological barriers differ between industry sectors and depending on the specific product. Technological barriers include the following:

- Inability to deliver high-quality remanufactured products. Limitations arise from the inability to recover materials due to the ineffectiveness of current recycling processes. For example, mobile phones contain about $16 worth of high-value metals, such as gold, silver or palladium, and only about $3 worth of these materials can be recovered with current recycling processes. Existing treatment technologies and processes of return product, component and material streams remain insufficient to effectively recycle existing products.
- Product designs currently on the market did not consider reverse streams and resulting disassembly into account meaning that many components or materials need to be destroyed when products are disassembled. This is especially applicable for products with long life spans but often also applies to other products, such as electronic appliances,

where the product is not necessarily designed to be recycled. Approaches of sustainable product design are often not widely applied.

- Waste materials are often contaminated or impure limiting the ability to recycle them. Instead, recylced materials often need to be diluted with virgin materials to obtain useful inputs for new products.
- Existing collection and pre-sorting systems are not effective or inefficient in sorting existing product return streams. More advanced recycling and recovery processes are needed.
- Recycling itself creates environmental effects through process steps, such as cleaning. These effects can reduce their environmental effectiveness overall.
- Many products are subject to fast technology development cycles. This applies especially in the electronics industry, where the pace of technological development has been increasing. Operators of reverse supply streams for reuse or recycle remain uncertain regarding the quantity and quality of future reverse streams. For example, volumes of valuable metals have been decreasing in electronic products while plastics have been increasing.

Market and economic barriers

Market and economic barriers often hinder the development or implementation of more circular approaches in practice. Existing barriers include the following:

- Low prices of virgin materials. This means that in many cases, it remains cheaper or easier to use virgin materials than more costly recycled materials.
- Distance between the places where waste is generated, collected and treated has to be relatively short to avoid high logistics costs. This means that in some areas it is not cost efficient to implement reverse chains and material streams.
- The sufficiency of reverse material streams can often not be guaranteed. One reason is that significant amounts of waste streams often disappear due to inefficient household sorting and recycling and unofficial exports. This limits the feasibility of processes in the reverse supply chain, which would rely on imported waste products to retain scale.
- Existing processes have been optimised to be cost efficient for individual companies. New process steps that would enable more efficient value recovery are seen to add costs.
- Developing new recovery processes or systems is typically associated with high up-front investment costs. Reversely, the effects are uncertain as new recovery systems would compete with other treatment options for the same (limited) reverse product flow.
- Volatility of material prices on global markets affects the cost-effectiveness of using materials from recycled products. For example, volatility of global metal prices and uncertainty of future price development affect the business case of using reverse material streams.

Regulatory barriers

Regulatory barriers relate to the influence that governmental and regulatory bodies have on organisational practice. The regulatory barriers on creating circular economy include the following:

- Regulations can have unintended consequences. For example, the US Toxic Substances Control Act creates a compliance burden that discourages companies from attempting to recycle electronic waste. Similarly, the toy manufacturer LEGO attempts to reuse plastic for their bricks (see Chapter 2), but the toy industry is highly regulated with regard to health and safety issues that make the use of recycled material very limited. Similar examples exist in the healthcare sector. Here, existing regulations can unintentionally discourage organisations to explore or implement solutions towards circular economy.

• Government inaction in combination with existing obstructing laws and regulation lacking global consensus can hinder organisations' engagement in circular practices as this would not be beneficial in comparison to the status quo.
• Regulatory uncertainty (i.e., organisations' lacking ability to predict future regulations and the timing of their introduction) creates difficulties in anticipating national legislative changes. The result is often inaction until uncertainty has been reduced.
• Existing regulations can have counteracting implications. For example, increasing plastic waste recycling targets and harmful substances regulation (persistent organic pollutants (POP) regulation) are not aligned.
• Organisations may lack incentives to engage with or invest in circular approaches. For example, market-based economic incentives are not sufficient to encourage producers to improve the recyclability of electrical and electronic equipment and hence improve the recyclability of these products. This requires additional instruments, including regulation.

Supply chain barriers

Many barriers to creating circular economy exist in the supply chain of organisations. Yet, it is typically the supply chain, where changes need to happen as described in the Box "Note: Supply chain must drive move to circular economy."

Note: Supply chain must drive move to circular economy

Current supply chains must transform to realise circular economy. A report by the logistics provider DHL stresses the central role that logistics solutions play in realising circularity in supply chains. Innovative logistics solutions, such as sustainable and re-usable packaging, and smart product return and collection solutions, enable optimised production volumes and materials, extended product life cycles, implementing new product-use models and new solutions for products' end-of-life.

Solutions need to be driven by different actors in the supply chain. Specifically, the DHL report highlights the critical role of consumers in driving circularity. Consumers signal demand through the amount of products and services purchased, and consumer behaviours determine if products are returned to the supply loop. Novel logistics solutions can form an enabler for sustainable consumer behaviour towards circular economy. For example, smart logistics solutions, such as multi-user repair warehouses, consolidated reverse logistics for returns, and recycling can enhance the rate of products returned into the supply stream.

Source: https://supplychaindigital.com/sustainability/dhl-says-supply-chain-must-drive-move-to-circular-economy; DHL White paper: Delivering on circularity: Pathways for fashion and consumer electronics, available from: https://www.dhl.com/global-en/home/insights-and-innovation/thought-leadership/white-papers/delivering-on-circularity.html

The supply chain barriers include the following:

- Established supply chains may be characterised by a lack of collaboration or even tensions between partners creating a lack of willingness to collaborate on new endeavours. For example, there may be strong competition between different organisations in the supply chain or a lack of trust. This creates a barrier to collaborating on circular projects and investments, which often require joint efforts from multiple supply chain partners.
- Supply chains (especially reverse ones) often involve triadic or network set-ups with often complex contractual arrangements. Governing these may be difficult. For example, sharing the costs and revenues between partners is often challenging. Similarly, many existing arrangements are based on short-term contracts based on economic incentives, prohibiting long-term collaborative investments.
- Required relationships may be missing. For example, many national recycling centres are not in direct contact with upstream supply chain partners, who might have the capabilities for reusing, remanufacturing or recycling the products, components or material.
- Many product changes have supply chain effects, which require addressing by external partners. For example, lighter plastic bottles (which save transport costs and emissions) can fool recycling separation systems, which were designed for heavier plastic bottles. Other materials, which may be designed to be more environmentally friendly (e.g., "green plastics," such as bio-derived polylactic acid – PLA), may not be recyclable at all.

Cultural barriers

Cultural barriers are often related to social habits and can arise from the following factors:

- Consumer awareness and interest may favour linear systems with regular replacements of products. Consumer habits, market resistance and transaction frictions may inhibit getting discarded objects to a pickup point or recycling centre. This can explain observed national differences in recycling streams – such as 77% of plastic waste being placed into recycling in Japan, while it is only 20% in the United States of America.
- Company culture can prohibit engagement in circular efforts. For example, return streams may be perceived as waste instead of a stream of valuable materials.
- Reaching circular economy may be perceived as too complex and difficult to attempt. First steps are not taken because the final goal is too far out of reach.

Overcoming barriers

Different supply chain partners can create an access point for motivating the transition into circularity. The Box "Note: Supply chain must drive move to circular economy" described the role that logistics providers can play in encouraging or even accelerating the transition towards circularity. Consumption is often placed at the forefront of drivers for overcoming the barriers listed above. This relates to the behaviours of consumers and customers in terms of consuming products and services as well as returning used products into reverse supply chains (The Box "Note: Consumption as access point for circular economy").

Note: Consumption as access point for circular economy

Consumption drives the entry of new products on the market and the amount of waste created. Especially the weeks leading up to major holidays, such as Christmas, can see a large spike in purchases of new products, including user electronics such as phones or tablets. This in turn leads to many usable products being discarded as waste. Especially sales campaigns such as Black Friday or Cyber Monday push new items into the market, replacing now unwanted older products. The campaign group Material Focus, for example, estimates that 5 million electrical items are thrown away or hoarded because of purchases made in the lead-up to Christmas. This estimate is based on a survey of 2,000 adults in the United Kingdom, which found that about 2.7 million unwanted electrical items are being disposed of on landfills, while an additional 2.2 million items are hoarded at home. This relates to a value of £160 million. Material Focus hence recommends that these unwanted products should be donated or recycled so they can be redistributed to people in need of these often still functioning items.

Source: https://theguardian.com/environment/2021/nov/26/e-waste-black-friday-uk-shoppers-donated-recycled-material-focus-campaign

Despite the importance typically placed on consumption, other supply chain actors can also drive or accelerate the transition towards circularity. Other influential actors are industry leaders. The Box "Example: Servitization as an access point for circular economy – follow-up on BWSC" describes how existing relationships and access points to used products in need of replacement can form a basis for transforming a supply chain towards circularity.

Example: Servitization as an access point for circular economy – follow-up on BWSC

Remanufacturing is one of the areas that Burmeister & Wain Scandinavian Contractor (BWSC) has identified to achieve significant sustainability effects for their energy plants in remote areas. BWSC has integrated sustainability in their corporate vision and has placed services at the core of achieving this vision. The company is exploring the sustainability effects of remanufacturing some of its exchanged parts after servicing the plants on site. To explore the possibility of remanufacturing parts, BWSC investigated both the economic and environmental impacts. Using data and insights available from their service business at a plant in Africa as well as data from their customers and suppliers based on long-term trusting relationships, BWSC conducted a life-cycle cost (LCC) and life-cycle analysis (LCA) for three exemplar parts that could improve sustainability performance. Such parts – including turbochargers, cylinder heads and plunger barrels – create most of their emissions and costs during manufacturing. Table 10.I outlines some of the assumptions underlying the calculations.

TABLE 10.1 Assumptions for comparing the economic and environmental effects of remanufacturing vs. replacing with new parts

New part	Remanufacture
Manufacturing: emissions and cost incurred through regular production of a first-generation part	Manufacturing: emissions and cost incurred through regular production of a first-generation part
Distribution: transport of the part from northern Europe to customer plant in Africa (based on actual values from 2020)	Distribution: transport of the part from northern Europe to customer plant in Africa (based on actual values from 2020); transport of used part from the customer plant in Africa to the remanufacturing plant in northern Europe and transport of remanufactured part from northern Europe to customer plant in Africa
Recycling: values gained from recycling the part	Remanufacturing: emissions and cost incurred through remanufacturing process to create second-generation part
Note: values are doubled to represent 1x first-generation and 1x second-generation part	Recycling: values gained from recycling second-generation part

Figure 10.1 presents the environmental and economic analyses for the three examples using data available from BWSC's own assessments and from customer and supplier operations. For all three chosen products, remanufacturing offers a clear improvement in terms of costs and emissions, leading to improved sustainability performance.

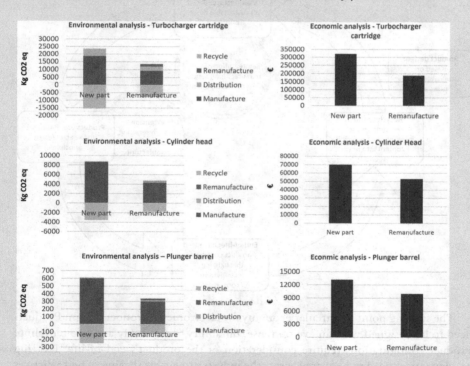

FIGURE 10.1 Emissions comparison of new parts and remanufactured parts.

Based on Bin, C.A. (2022). The role of services to increase sustainability of power generation equipment. Master's thesis at Technical University of Denmark, Department of Technology, Management and Economics.

Incentives can also be given by governments through regulations (such as the Waste Electrical and Electronic Equipment (WEEE)) and international organisations (such as the UN or the World Economic Forum (WEF)). The Box "Note: A new circular vision for electronics – Time for a global reboot" describes this in more detail.

Note: A new circular vision for electronics – Time for a global reboot

Many international organisations – individually and in collaboration – push a more aggressive shift towards circularity. For example, the Platform for Accelerating the Circular Economy (PACE) provides a hub for more than 70 leaders and 20 communities from different public and private sectors to accelerate change. They focus specifically on four thematic areas with most potential, namely electronics, plastics, fashion and textile and food and agriculture. The aim is to establish a common set of metrics enabling accurate measurement and hence monitoring of progress towards circular economy.

Focusing on electronic waste, the WEF outlines a circular vision for electronics. Created as a collaborative effort between heads of UN agencies with the WEF and the World Business Council for Sustainable Development, their report outlines how changes in product design, manufacturing of the devices and the whole supply chain can create circularity as shown in the figure below.

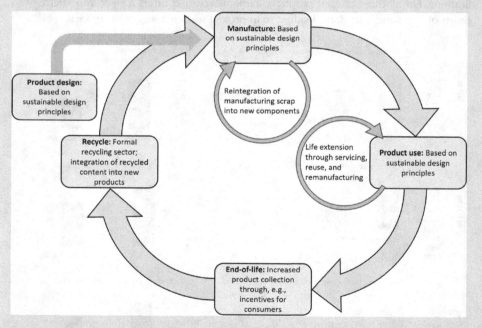

The starting point for circular economy for electronics is product design. Products need to be designed with an eye on reuse, durability, disassembly and safe recycling. Product configurations require consideration of the product's end-of-life. Existing good practices need to be shared across the industry to enable sharing of best practices and collaboration. Similarly, buy-back or return systems offered by producers of electronics would incentivise customers financially and ensure that data is handled appropriately. This would form a first step towards the creation of a system for advanced recycling and recapturing of materials.

The ultimate aim is closed-loop production, where all old products are collected and their materials and components reintegrated into new products. The report recognised the importance of manufacturers, consumers, policy makers and other parties in achieving this aim. In addition, the recycling sector will require updating to ensure that recycled materials are of sufficient quality to be used in new products. Investment into "urban mining" to implement technology that allows extracting metals and minerals from e-waste offers huge benefits. This will not only mitigate the adverse effects of electronic waste but also create economic growth and decent work through creating safe and responsible forward and reverse supply chains.

The report also explores the option of offering electronic devices as a service whereby consumers gain access to the use of the device without purchasing its ownership. In a similar fashion as streaming apps, such as Netflix and Spotify, replace the need to own devices, such as DVDs, CDs and tapes, consumer ownership of electronic devices could be replaced through services. Existing leasing and rental models, where a consumer pays a monthly fee to gain access to a smartphone and upgrades, already exist. These models can be used to incentivise manufacturers to ensure that returned devices are entered into the reverse supply chain through reuse or recycle. Manufacturer would be perfectly placed to increase the value of the product for as long as possible, including extending the useful life of a device; repair and maintain them when required; and laminate waste and reduce the impact of electronic devices on the environment.

Notes

1 https://www.statista.com/statistics/530481/largest-dump-sites-worldwide/
2 European Commission. (2011). Roadmap to a resource efficient Europe. Communication from the Commission to the European Parliament, the Council, the European Economic and Social Committee and the Committee of the Regions, EU COM 571, available from: https://ec.europa.eu/environment/resource_efficiency/about/roadmap/index_en.ht; p. 7.
3 Ellen MacArthur Foundation. (2015). Growth within: A circular economy vision for a competitive Europe. In: collaboration with McKinsey Center for Business and Environment, available from: https://emf.thirdlight.com/link/8izw1qhml4ga-404tsz/@/preview/1?o
4 Ellen MacArthur Foundation. (2015). Growth within: A circular economy vision for a competitive Europe. In collaboration with McKinsey Center for Business and Environment, available from: https://emf.thirdlight.com/link/8izw1qhml4ga-404tsz/@/preview/1?o; p. 23.
5 Ellen MacArthur Foundation. (2015). Growth within: A circular economy vision for a competitive Europe. In collaboration with McKinsey Center for Business and Environment, available from: https://emf.thirdlight.com/link/8izw1qhml4ga-404tsz/@/preview/1?o; p. 23.
6 See, for example, Mahmoum Gonbadi, A., Genovese, A., Sgalambro, A., (2021). Closed-loop supply chain design for the transition towards a circular economy: A systematic literature review of methods, applications and current gaps. *Journal of Cleaner Production*, vol. 323, pp. 129101. https://doi.org/10.1016/j.jclepro.2021.129101
7 Ellen MacArthur Foundation. (2012). *Towards the Circular Economy: Economic and Business Rationale for an Accelerated Transition*, January, available from: ellenmacarthurfoundation.org; https://www.ellenmacarthurfoundation.org/circular-economy/what-is-the-circular-economy

8 The specific barriers have been reported in different sector-specific studies and may hence apply only to these specific sectors. Based on Aminoff, A., Sundqvist-Andberg, H. (2021). Constraints leading to system-level lock-ins—the case of electronic waste management in the circular economy. *Journal of Cleaner Production*, vol. 322, no. 129029. https://doi.org/10.1016/j.jclepro.2021.129029; Kirchherr, J., Piscicellia, L., Boura, R., Kostense-Smit, E., Mullerb, J., Huibrechtse-Truijensb, A., Hekkert, M. (2018). Barriers to the circular economy: Evidence from the European Union (EU). In: *Ecological Economics*, 150, pp. 264–272; Wang, J.X., Burke, H., Zhang, A. (2022). Overcoming barriers to circular product design. *International Journal of Production Economics*, vol. 243, pp. 108346. https://doi.org/10.1016/j.ijpe.2021.108346

CASE 3

Novo Nordisk – Environmental and social sustainability in supply chains

Novo Nordisk, as the world's largest producer of insulin products (such as the insulin pen, Figure C3.1), takes its responsibility for social and environmental sustainability seriously. The company has implemented an ambitious sustainability strategy which targets their supply chain activities. This strategy has the goal of reducing CO_2 emissions from transportation, enabling global access to care through supporting local supply chain capabilities to countries within pharmaceutical supply chains and a take-back programme for used insulin pens. Through these initiatives, Novo Nordisk has not only accepted the social responsibility of operating in the pharmaceutical industry but is also on target for reaching its goal of net zero emissions in their value chain by 2045.

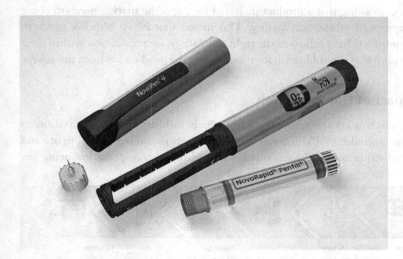

FIGURE C3.1 NovoPen 4.

DOI: 10.4324/9781003345077-16

Background

Novo Nordisk A/S is a healthcare company operating in the pharmaceutical industry. Founded in 1923, it designs, manufactures and distributes products to treat diabetes and other related diseases, such as obesity. It supplies nearly half of the insulin on the planet through products such as the insulin pen. Novo Nordisk is a globally operating company headquartered just outside of Copenhagen, Denmark. It is the world's largest producer of insulin with a global market share of about 50%. It produces insulin and medical equipment for distribution in 16 countries and is available in the healthcare markets of 169 countries.

The company has implemented an ambitious plan for sustainable business through a socially and environmentally responsible strategy. It estimates that, based on current nutrition and healthcare patterns, about 736 million people will have diabetes globally in 2045, and about half of the population in many high-income countries will suffer from it by 2050. To counter this development, Novo Nordisk aims not only at treating diabetes but at helping societies to prevent type 2 diabetes by providing access and affordable care to vulnerable patients in every country. Furthermore, Novo Nordisk is the first pharmaceutical company to use only renewable power in all its production facilities. In 2021, it defined an even more ambitious aim: achieving net zero across their entire value chain by 2045.

The insulin value chain

Once a new product is handed over from the research and development (R&D) department, the Operations in Product Supply department manages the supply of all products within Novo Nordisk. This involves activities such as the purchase of input materials, assembly, packing and distribution (see Figure C3.2).

One of the primary sources of Novo Nordisk's CO_2 emissions is transportation, both between production sites and the final market. Pharmaceutical products need to undergo tight regulatory approval within each market, and approval often involves specific production facilities and processes, meaning that a product intended for a specific market needs to come from a specific pre-approved production facility. This means that Novo Nordisk needs to prove both that their products have followed the tight regulations for production within their specific target markets and that the cold chain for transporting the product has been unbroken.

Reducing the impact of transportation

Novo Nordisk commands a complex supply chain which includes the transportation of active pharmaceutical ingredients (APIs), raw materials, pre-assembled components and packaging among production sites and from suppliers, resulting in transportation being the

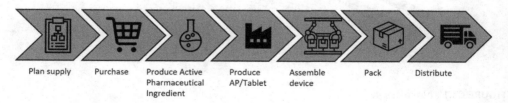

Plan supply   Purchase   Produce Active Pharmaceutical Ingredient   Produce AP/Tablet   Assemble device   Pack   Distribute

FIGURE C3.2 Extent of Novo's operations and supply management.

main source of Novo Nordisk's CO_2 emissions. Cold chain regulations constrain many of the transportation and logistics decisions (Box 1).

Novo Nordisk uses three modes of transport: road, air and sea (Table C3.1). Air shipments contribute most to the costs while making up only about one fifth of shipping volume. In contrast, road shipments have the largest volume but make up only a quarter of the costs. Novo aims to reduce CO_2 emissions through avoiding airfreight and adopting green transport solutions. The company is not currently using rail transport, but it is one of the modes of transport the company is investigating, including the possibility of gaining regulatory approval for its use in Novo's cold chains. Novo Nordisk has implemented an internal transport policy aimed at creating transparency and visibility in the control of transport.

One of the main investments concerns the digitalisation of transportation to enable oversight of temperature data and to investigate when and how temperatures vary. Between 2016 and 2017, Novo Nordisk developed dashboards for their shipments which display an overview of cold chain performance, including an assessment of lanes and routes. This enables performance optimisation in routing decisions for their shipments (e.g., reducing handling or avoiding specific terminals). From here, Novo Nordisk is working on an integrated tool to optimise product transport by offering a temperature logger system, weather data and data concerning their local strategic partnerships with logistics providers. In 2019, the company implemented a lane performance management system to minimise unnecessary excursions as well as logger use optimisation to reduce the number of temperature loggers used in each shipment, optimise transport packaging and proactively avoid or reduce product scrap by applying the right packaging solutions to the specific transport needs.

Social sustainability and responsibility: Reaching vulnerable patients

Giving healthcare access to vulnerable patients (e.g., refugees or displaced people who have lost their homes and family to wars or unrest) is a priority for Novo Nordisk. For reasons such as climate change, violence, persecution and socioeconomic conflict, 70.8 million people have been forced to flee their homes, and 3.5 million are expected to have diabetes while having little to no access to healthcare. Novo Nordisk defines "access and affordability" as one of the three pillars of their social responsibility strategy. By 2030, the company wants to have reached 1 million vulnerable patients.

Many of these vulnerable patients are located in geographic and geopolitical areas characterised by instability. Distributing medicines such as insulin, however, requires cold chains (i.e., controlled temperature environments to keep the medicine safe). Part of the pharmaceutical company's social responsibility programme was to enable access to insulin, which required actions on three fronts.

First, Novo Nordisk needed to reduce the lead time of producing insulin to enable responsive supply based on suddenly emerging needs. To do this, they made process

TABLE C3.1 Novo Nordisk's current use of modes of transportation

	Road	Air	Sea
Volume	58%	21%	21%
Cost	26%	55%	19%

improvements, including optimisation of product supply procedures. For example, they delayed the identification of the end market of a product, thus reducing the need to customise production and packaging for a specific market. In sum, these efforts resulted in the product lead time being reduced from 12 weeks to 6–8 weeks.

Second, Novo improved its internal processes for donations. This included identifying and rerouting donatable products to vulnerable patients. A donatable product is one that still has sufficient shelf life left to be used by patients safely. However, these products cannot take the "usual" supply lines anymore because of global mandatory guidelines for the remaining shelf life of products entering local markets. In addition to improving the monitoring of product shelf life in their global distribution channels and rerouting products to vulnerable patients, Novo established long-term agreements with humanitarian non-governmental organisations (NGOs) and their wholesalers.

Third, Novo Nordisk engages directly in building supply chain capacities in low-income countries. Many low-income countries present specific obstacles for the local distribution of pharmaceutical products, especially those requiring cold chains (see Table C3.2). Novo Nordisk works in these locations to build supply chain capacities. For example, they piloted a partnership with the Africa Resource Centre (ARC) in Kenya. Another example is a project in Ethiopia, where they work with Addis Ababa University and a network of local public and private stakeholders to educate supply chain managers locally. This includes education on how to handle pharmaceuticals in humanitarian settings. These activities are aimed at establishing a sustainable healthcare supply chain programme to ensure a continuous and equitable supply of medicine to patients in Ethiopia.

These efforts enabled Novo Nordisk to donate insulin for 200,000 people in 2019, for which they were thanked by the United Nations.

Novo Nordisk's take-back programme: Solving the end-of-life challenge for products

Novo Nordisk implemented a "Circular for Zero" policy to reduce the impact of their supply chain activities on the environment. However, most medical consumption products, such as insulin pens, are currently single use. An insulin pen is a small device (see Figure C3.1) that allows a patient to inject the correct amount of insulin directly into their bloodstream, thus reducing the need for interaction with a healthcare professional and enabling a higher quality of life for patients. However, such products pose significant challenges for sustainability as they are typically single use. The reason for this is direct patient contact or in this case penetration, which means that when used, these products may be contaminated and pose a risk of cross-contamination. As a result, most of these single-use healthcare products currently end up in landfills.

TABLE C3.2 Typical obstacles for supply chain capacities in low-income countries

Obstacles
Political unrest and instability undermining personal safety
Military regimes which control access to local infrastructure and markets
Underdeveloped logistic networks which limit or undermine guaranteed cold chains for local distribution

In December 2020, Novo Nordisk piloted a take-back scheme for their insulin pens in their native Denmark. In three major Danish cities, Copenhagen, Kolding and Aarhus, it launched a take-back programme which enabled patients to return their used insulin pens. The entry point into reverse logistics are the local pharmacies that patients use when acquiring a new insulin pen. This programme is voluntary as early focus groups with patients have shown that they did not want to receive any incentives for returning their used insulin pens but saw it as an obligation to society.

This arrangement requires collaboration between a large set of partners. In total, 15 partners, including wholesalers and municipalities, signed a mutual agreement, which enabled the launch of the take-back programme. Through this scheme, they achieved a return rate of 13% in six months and aimed to increase this to 30% within the first year. In 2022, they are implementing similar programmes in other countries, including the United Kingdom, the United States of America and China.

INDEX

Printed in the United States
by Baker & Taylor Publisher Services